Paving the Way for Peace

The Living Philosophies of Bishnois and Jains

Herma Brockmann and Renato Pichler

Originals
(an imprint of Low Price Publications)
Delhi-110052

Distributed by
D.K. Publishers Distributors (P) Ltd.
4834/24, Ansari Road, Darya Ganj,
New Delhi-110002
Phones: 51562573-77
e-mail: dkpd@del3.vsnl.net.in
visit us at: www.dkpd.com

German Version: A Vegi-Verlag Book, Neukirch-Egnach, Switzerland

German Edition Published November 2001
First English Edition Published 2004
Translated by: Herma Brockmann

ISBN 81-88629-23-5

Published by
Originals
(an imprint of Low Price Publications)
A-6, Nimri Commercial Centre,
Near Ashok Vihar Phase-IV, Delhi-110052
Phones: 27401672, 27452453
e-mail: lpp@nde.vsnl.net.in
visit us at: www.lppindia.com

Photos:Bishnoi-Chapter and cover: Harsh Vardhan
Jains-Chapter: from the Book "Jainism - A Pictorial Guide to the Religion of Non-Violence", with the kind permission of Mrs. Martha Titze, widow of the author
Cover photos:front: Sugan Singh Bishnoi, wife of Hanuman Singh Bishnoi, member of WWF-Rajasthan-Committee, Back: Black Buck

Printed at: **D K Fine Art Press P Ltd.,** Delhi-110052

PRINTED IN INDIA

Contents

Thank you! It has been great!

Just like any journey starts with the very first step, every book finds its beginning in the first word; and in both cases it is not clear whether and how the ultimate goal can be reached and which obstacles may obstruct the way. Under uncertain conditions like that, fellow travellers not only offer welcome company but sometimes also show directions, point to dangers, warn about detours and motivate when the road seems blocked. We were privileged by so much support that we would like to thank all of our companions, especially Christel and Toby Westoby, Vasudev Murthy, Dilip Bafna, Josie Wendt, Ajit Benadi, Bernie Wright and Fredy Forster. Thank you all! Your support has been of crucial importance to us!

Herma Brockmann and Renato Pichler

Foreword

Have you ever wondered that when walking in forests you almost never meet deer, wild boar or squirrels? This is not because they are extinct in our regions. The very popular explanation that these animals are shy and genetically obliged to flee from humans is nothing but a soothing excuse. All explanations seem welcome to explain why we are not to blame.

We have adopted the idea of, first of all, not being part of nature and, secondly, of having to squeeze out of nature what we can get. Whenever we wish to observe "wild" animals more closely, we do not go out into natural surroundings but visit a zoo, a circus or a reserve where animals have no chance of escape. Or we make do with the so-called domestic animals that, according to present laws, can be treated as property and are at the entire mercy of people who consider themselves to be their "owners".

But is there really no other way? Do we really have to resign ourselves to these substitutes when trying to achieve more harmony with our animal brothers? Indeed, our experience does not seem to indicate other possibilities because throughout known history it always has been a fact that wild animals were encountered only when they could be captured, locked up or killed.

However, it is the intention of this book to prove that this state of affairs is by no means a fixed law of nature and that, on the contrary, even the shyest of animals, like wild gazelles, show an interest to approach us and play with our children.

In describing the following examples we would like to invite people to re-think their deep-rooted pre-conceptions and consider abandoning our deadly ways with nature. If we continue upsetting the ecological balance by the insidious killing of peaceful animals (called hunting), we are in the long run not only harming them but, at the same time, our human souls. No wonder that under present conditions hardly any animal dares getting close to us because they experience each and every day that they have in fact been excluded when we boast about charity and non-aggression.

Certainly, a lot of water will pass under the bridge before humans overcome the trinity-partition of their animal world, namely pets, domesticated and wild animals. Many an old custom will have to be reconsidered and changed. Not only the most direct form of humiliation, which is to consider our fellow-beings as nothing but food-resources (expressed by the consumption of meat) or test-objects in animal experiments, but also our hobbies (horse or dog-races, bullfights) need a general new orientation. The animals are ready for a peaceful co-existence that would bring blessings to both sides: what about us?

Renato Pichler

*President of the **Swiss Union for Vegetarianism***

Chapter 1

The Bishnois

"The greatness of a society is shown by the way it treats its animals"

Mahatma Gandhi

The Khan Scandal

"Anybody who tries to even kill a bird or cut a tree in our area, can't get away easily"

Sukhram of Guda Bishnoi

Had the idolized Indian film-celebrities just lost their feeling for the difference between fantasy and reality or had the making of the new brutal action-packed film led to a kind of blood thirst? Or did Salman Khan and his friends want to imitate the feudal lords of long ago who had their importance judged by the number of kills they brought back from hunting excursions? Or had, in the autumn of 1998, the arrogant youngsters just considered themselves to be able to get away with something for which a normal citizen can be locked up for seven years?

Whatever their reasons might have been: During their breaks in shooting a film in Rajasthan, Salman Khan and his friends allegedly went out shooting animals instead or, just for fun, chased herds of terrified gazelles to exhaustion.

After one of these unfortunate blunders even the kitchen personnel of the luxury hotel in Jodhpur, where the group was accommodated, were called out of bed at two o'clock in the morning with the order to prepare the forbidden meat - and thereby making themselves guilty as well.

Had the gun-crazy stars really lost their marbles?

Although hunting everywhere is considered as just a banal event, which surprisingly is even called "a sport", the situation was different in this case because the law was broken twice: First of all, strictly protected game was killed, i.e. graceful Indian antelopes Chinkara as well as rare Black Bucks, and, secondly, this occurred right in the heart of the Bishnoi-region! There were many eyewitnesses.

But, just as a straw may eventually break the camel's back, it so happened that the bloodstained jeep had transported the shooting party once too often.

On 1 October, the rich and powerful youngsters had again killed two animals when inhabitants of a village, which is situated in the proximity of Jodhpur, caught them red-handed. The furious villagers immediately pressed charges and so the jet-set group was arrested a few days later, on 12 October. They were accused of killing threatened animals in a protected area of Rajasthan. It was for this reason that Khan experienced the doubtful honour of being the first person to be kept in the state forest department's custody since the Wildlife Protection Act in 1972 came into force.

Indian Gazelles can be seen around desert Bishnoi villages

Whilst his friends were immediately released against bail, Salman Khan was held for a week. Even though food from the luxury hotel was brought in by his brother, Khan had to make do with armed guards at his door instead of subservient waiters. But the accused remained unimpressed and denied all charges against him. He even made one of his lawyers take the offensive: "The statements made against my client are all open to question. Either they have been made by people also accused of crimes with their own offenses to consider, or they have been made by the Bishnoi, people whose attraction to wildlife — even worship of it — twists their thinking."

Actually, in the beginning everything really seemed to develop in the interest of the celebrities. An official veterinary even acknowledged in his postmortem report that the animals had died because of "leaping" and "overeating". The animals were buried where they had been found and the case seemed to be fizzling out and thereby reinforcing the obvious carelessness of the famous prisoner.

The Bishnois were seething with rage and made, by means of demonstrations and strikes, their feelings about this sacrilege crystal clear. Of course, the media loves such juicy scandals and especially so in connection with superstar Khan. There were so many detailed reports concerning this matter that, under increasing public pressure, the autopsy of the killed animals had to be repeated. They were excavated again and this time a team of veterinarians made a renewed investigation. Their result did not surprise anybody: shot!

Things were getting unpleasant for Salman Khan! Now the common truth that the rich and famous can get away with murder did not hold any longer and, furthermore, the noisy Bishnoi indignation had reached offices where sensitized politicians paid a lot of attention to the echoing turmoil: Elections for the state assembly were pending and the Bishnoi votes were liable to influence the outcome in six to seven constituencies in Rajasthan. Thus, the ruling BJP Party, as well as the opposition Congress Party, excelled themselves with demands for stern action in the interest of this particular religious community and their admirable philosophy.

Of course, the Bishnois themselves, for whom the killing of animals is a sin, also demanded strong punishment for offenders. They were full of bitterness when they pointed out that these animals, who had become tame by constant human contact, had been killed at a holy place in their region: in the proximity of Guda Bishnoi. In this area, many of their ancestors had given their lives centuries ago when protesting against the felling of trees.

But whoever had hoped that this poaching incident would sooner or later disappear from the headlines, and the situation eventually calm down, had not counted on the lasting and righteous indignation of conservationists. Especially the Tourism and Wildlife Society of India in Jaipur took a prominent stance and even called for the boycott of the poacher-film stars.

The success of the just finished Khan-film seemed compromised so that the bosses in the Indian movie-center (with the interesting name "Bollywood") became jumpy at all the negative publicity. A producer: "How could they have been so irresponsible. I do not know what exactly the guys have done but certainly one would have expected a bit more sense of responsibility."

The World Wildlife Fund reacted quickly and exchanged a photo of Khan from their 1999 calendar with that of another film star, although some series had already been printed. According to a report in the "Hindu", after this ugly affair the WWF no longer appreciated being associated with Mr. Khan.

The "Hindu" daily, in an editorial under the heading "Desert Storm", asked the government of Rajasthan to "make all effort in clarifying what really happened and then punish the culprits accordingly. That will show, better than anything else, that nobody, however rich and famous, may destroy deliberately the precious animal life of our country."

The "Indian Express" from Bombay wrote about the problem: "Whatever the case, there can be no disputing that the threat to wildlife is too real to be glossed over. Every specimen of wildlife is a symbol of our biodiversity and needs to be protected. This is possible only if public consciousness is aroused so that it does not let the Salman Khans who shoot to kill go scot free."

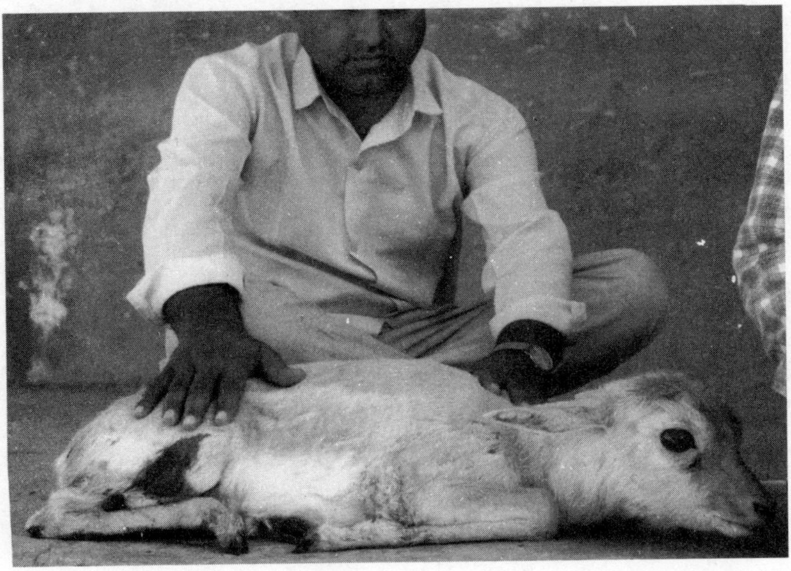

After an attack by dogs, a young Indian Gazelle is nursed back to health

Maybe in this case it was not the public but the consciousness of the Bishnois that had been "aroused" enough! And, in connection with this particular scandal, many contemporaries learned for the first time about the existence of this unique religious community of dedicated conservationists and their amazing philosophy of a harmonious togetherness of humans with Flora and Fauna.

Pacifists on the Warpath

"What makes me proud is that the next generation is even more committed to nature than we are."

Bana Ram

Now, all of a sudden, the Bishnois found themselves in the limelight even though they wished nothing better than living in peace, following their convictions. Since their courage received unprecedented media attention, they were unintentionally starring as the heroes in an eco-drama, offering readers the possibility to witness a fight between good and bad, right and wrong. After all, who does not enjoy the interplay of forces between many little Davids and one powerful Goliath?

Helas, as always in most court-cases and including this one, existing hopes for a speedy settlement and following punishment have not been justified. Even at the time that this book was written, which after all is some years later, the file "Khan" still cannot be closed.

But there is one consolation all the same: This scandal and the prospect of a severe prison-sentence can be considered as a deterrent. And, for this reason alone, the black bucks as well as the Chinkaras and other animals in the Bishnoi-areas might enjoy a bit more security, at least for the moment.

But who are these people who have lived for centuries in great harmony with a demanding and harsh environment and whose unique philosophy has recently made headlines, almost by chance and in a very unusual manner? What are their motives for collectively going on the warpath in the interest of a few killed animals?

And what did actually happen on this fateful night of 1 October 1998 when the cocky young film stars ventured out into an area, which they better had not entered? According to the report in several newspapers it must have been something like this: It was around midnight when the villagers of Kankani near Guda Bishnoi were woken up by shots. They jumped out of bed with the grim intention of protecting their beloved black bucks against some crazy, trigger-happy poachers. But they were too late.

"I saw their jeep race by, and my head filled up with anger," said Prahlad Ram, aged 68. "We all began to shout and scramble. They had already killed the Chinkaras. These animals are sacred to us, and we consider their lives even more important than our own."

But at least two of the villagers managed, on their scooters, to get close enough to the jeep of the poachers to recognize their number-plates. These scouts also discovered that they had to do with the famous Salman Khan but the fact of confronting celebrities did not calm their fury. Just the opposite!

"No man, no matter how powerful, should be above the law. Had we caught him, we would have beaten him severely," confirmed the tall and slender Choka Ram.

In this context it must be mentioned that a beating is the favoured Bishnoi method of justice after having caught those tangled up with the law. In spite of many official reminders they still are inclined to take justice into their own fists because of their deep mistrust regarding the normal legal systems. It is even stated that Salman Khan enjoyed the chance of a narrow escape in that, after his discovery, he managed to get away unharmed. After all, the Bishnoi people are not only without any fear when defending their protégés, they are just as determined in their rage when discovering offenders.

Here are some examples:

In 1995 they prevented the take off of an Air Force helicopter after the crew had been hunting whilst airborne.

In October 1996 the Bishnois confronted a group of poachers with the intention of protecting an Indian Gazelle. One of the defenders was shot and died while being transported to hospital. According to the Bishnoi philosophy he became a martyr.

The Bishnois believe that all forms of life enjoy the same rights and that humans dying in the process of defending helpless animals or trees have deserved their place in paradise immediately. Through the killing of Nihal Chand Bishnoi, the sad fact of increased poaching was brought to public knowledge. Assurances of help were given and the widow of the victim even received a visit of WWF- Rajasthan Committee Member, Mr. Hanuman Singh Bishnoi.

In 1998 the white-clad "People of Vengeance" severely beat up an officer whom they had caught hunting.

In 2000, Ganga Ram Bishnoi fell to bullets of poachers in a village between Jodhpur and Osian. Financial help was offered to his widow by Mr. Harsh Vardhan.

Poachers in Rajasthan are wary of falling into the hands of Bishnois who are by no means choosy when they want to get their messages across and, in this context, have developed quite ingenuous methods. So when one day they caught an Indian Air Force captain hunting, they stripped him and forced him to lie down and roast on the hot sand in the middle of summer.

But also with the members of a neighbouring tribe the Bishnois got into trouble after those were suspected to have killed more than twenty Chinkaras and some peacocks, national animals of India, near the village Sanwatsar in the Churu District. Furious animal protectors cordoned off the local police station and forced fifteen arrests and later even the suspense of some police officers who had not prevented the massacre.

A Black Buck near Duga Bishnoi where the film stars committed their poaching crime

According to Indian press reports, the Bishnois now demand weapons because of all these incidents and illegal activities going on around them. Without official help they want to be in a position to protect themselves and the animals who are seeking shelter in their area. According to their philosophy, gentleness is first priority but, at the same time, they wish to stand up against incursions and sacrileges - using all possible means.

It is against this background that it becomes understandable why, for centuries, Bishnoi-people have sacrificed their lives in order to protect that of animals. But the Bishnois do not stop there! They even let themselves be decapitated when trying to prevent the felling of trees.

Amrita's Sacrifice

"We believe that whatever you do in this life, you pay for it in the next birth"

Teja Ram

It was in the year 1730 when the Maharaja Abhay Singh of Jodhpur needed wood for the construction of a new fortress. Since the Bishnois neither obeyed the demand for the delivery of timber nor made any payments instead, the ruler sent his soldiers out into the villages with the order to chop down Khejri trees (*Prosopis cineraria*). These trees, which prosper even under extremely harsh conditions, have always been worshipped by the Bishnois - and in appreciation offer them shade, food, building material, humid soils, protection and clean air.

Trunk and bark of a Khejri tree in Thar desert

When Amrita Devi heard of the imminent danger, she hurried, followed by relatives and neighbours, to the place of the tragedy, named Khejarli (translated: place at which the Khejri tree grows) and tried to prevent the soldiers from what they had come to do. However, when all reasoning failed, she hugged the first tree to be cut in order to protect it. The soldiers made short work of her and beheaded the woman, whose last words would become history: "sir saanthe runkh reho to bhi sasto jaan" (A chopped head is cheaper than a felled tree).

Although the soldiers had warned that anyone intending to stay in their way would share the fate of Amrita, her three daughters followed her example and were also killed. Men, women and children stepped forward, embraced the trees and let themselves be axed to death. One after the other died: Andoji, Virto, Vanial, Chaboji and Udoji, followed by Kanhoji, Kishoji and Dayarayaji. ....

The terrible message spread like wild fire, so that people from eighty-three different surrounding villages rushed in, ready for the extreme sacrifice - to lay down their own lives for trees.

When the Maharaja heard the cries of witnesses of the massacre, who had run to his court, he went himself to Khejarli and stopped the tragedy but by then it had already cost the lives of 363 Bishnois. The ruler was moved so deeply and so impressed by the dramatic non-violent protest that he promised to honour the conviction of the Bishnois in future. He forbade hunting and woodcutting in their area by means of a law, which is still valid today.

In memory of this bloody event, which is recorded in history as "the utmost sacrifice of Khejarli", every year a number of Khejri acacias are planted there. But apart from this particular celebration, the creation of groves became one of the most important religious obligations from that day on.

Even if the legend of Amrita seems without parallel in the history of nature-protection and demonstrates most adequately the potential scope of the Bishnoi spirit of self-sacrifice, this woman and her family members and friends were far from being the only ones to give their own lives for their convictions. Over the centuries again and again followers of this faith have sacrificed themselves for the protection of animals as well as trees.

The first self sacrifice of this kind is said is to have taken place in the year 1604 in the village of Ramsari in the proximity of Jodhpur: Two Bishnoi women named Karma and Gora let themselves be decapitated in protest against the felling of trees - in Indian history these are the first known self sacrifices (*sakas*) in the interest of trees. Nothing is known about the culprits, but the Bishnoi legends even now glow with lyric narrations about Karma and Gora, who are worshipped as an ever-flowing source of moral strength.

A further incident of a similar nature occurred 1643 in Polawas near Merta. When trees were cut for a celebration honoring the goddess Holi, a Bishnoi committed suicide in protest.

The Khejri trees have always been special friends to these people. Therefore many a legends speaks of those martyrs who gave their lives for their protection: Self-sacrifice is accepted in this society as a possible last way out. However, even for us who are upset about the endless destruction of forests everywhere in the world, this unique attitude nevertheless remains incomprehensible.

The quiet village Khejarli still exists today and is situated about 30 km south of Jodhpur. A tarred road leads into the place, which consists of an accumulation of scattered huts and a pond. A small structure — they call it temple — reminds of the 363 Bishnois, whose demonstration of altruism seems to still inspire the India of today. Indian Gazelles and Black Bucks roam around this shrine of mass self-sacrifice denoting the fact that animals and vegetation are safe in this region. For Bishnois reside here!

Memorial for 363 Bishnoi people who sacrificed their lives for trees hundreds of years ago

One could even assume that these sacrifices led Mahatma Gandhi to understand the extent to which simple people can be ready for resistance. If only they believe strongly enough in something, even the most brutal power will become instable when confronted with such stern determination. His philosophy of civilian disobedience could have been inspired by Khejarli!

Probably the oldest Khejri tree with a temple (Peepasar)

In addition, also the other places of "*sakas*", i.e. Ramsari and Polawas in the heart of the Bishnoi area, can still be visited today. In that region one discovers countless Khejri trees next to an impressive number of the most diverse shrubs and bushes. Nobody is allowed to tamper with these plants! Even newcomers know how unpleasant the Bishnois can become in case of encroachments.

The question of such motivation, capable of even overcoming the instinct of self-preservation, can probably only be understood in the presence of an extremely stable moral foundation. This extraordinary steel base was poured many centuries ago by someone who himself had just survived a famine.

The Seer Jambeshwar

"Show people the light"

More than five hundred years ago (1452), the seer was born in the village of Peepasar in the Nagpur District of Rajasthan. He belonged to a martial caste and moved later to Mukham (Bikaner District), where he died in 1537 at the age of 85 years. Today a massive temple at Mukam reminds of him, in which, however, in agreement with the principles and traditions of the Bishnois, no relics are to be found. Instead the building is surrounded by an impressive variety of domestic trees, in which trusting Chinkaras and black bucks amble. It goes without saying that in this part of the world hunting is considered as a deadly sin.

Already as a child Jambeshwar was extraordinary because of his evident thoughtfulness and unusual reaction which attracted the attention of people around him. Furthermore a daily contact with animals led to an ever-growing bonding with them.

Then in 1476 tragedy struck and pushed his life into a completely different direction: Drought hit the homeland of the 25 year old who witnessed with horror how people on their desperate quest for food

Jambeshwar has been teaching here for some months (Jodhpur)

killed almost all animals and cut down all trees. Desolation, emptiness and hopelessness spread fast, hunger and misery followed and drove many people out of Rajasthan.

Jambeshwar did not flee, but he went into isolation in order to meditate about the traumatic events. During his life as a hermit he eventually experienced a vision, the truth of which will nowadays be acknowledged by all scientific research: only a respectful co-existence of humans and nature can prevent misery and disaster.

That was how a philosophy was born that is second to none as far as a worldly-practical emphasis is concerned and which at the same time impresses by its wisdom to unite Hindu and Islamic elements. Thus the Bishnois worship Jambeshwar as their only God considering him to be the incarnation of Lord Vishnu. They, however, bury their dead like Muslims who return the bodies to the holy earth.

The Seer accepted the challenge of convincing his fellow men of the blessings of a considerate and caring contact with nature and by that created a new way of thinking. During his many years as preacher he actually succeeded in getting this "green" message across. Furthermore he rather quickly found followers who turned his lectures and teachings into songs and also reported of miracles he was said to have achieved.

Jambeshwar lived and died here. A memorial in Mukam

The teachings of Jambeshwar are based on laws, which stress the importance of virtues such as self-discipline, honesty and non-violence. This way of thinking brought about the 29 rules from which the name of the religion eventually derived i.e. Bishnoi (*Bish-noi* stands for '29').

Life and deeds of this religious founder, who never married, were praised by his contemporary Udoji Nain who was the only one to leave a written basis of the sermons of Jambeshwar. It is stated that Jambeshwar was a child for seven years, a cowboy for 27 and a holy preacher for the remainder of his long life: a God of the people. Wherever he appeared, houses of meditation were built some of which still exist as temples, among others in Mukam, Samrathal, Peepasar, Lohawat and Jamba.

Particularly touching in these documents is the fact that during his wanderings the Seer created groves everywhere such as the still flowering Khejri plantation in Rotu, a village near the road between Nagaur and Didwana. But Jambeshwar also planted trees like the one in Lodipur in the proximity of Moradabad in Uttar Pradesh where even nowadays people gather at special festive occasions to honour their spiritual leader.

If one considers the life story of Jambeshwar, his ban regarding the cutting of flowering trees or even chopping off branches and his command to protect them at all times and cost cannot come as a surprise.

Chinkara Gazelle in a holy grove between Mukam and Samrathal Dhora

While also other tribes in the world adhere to sound ecological rules and practice sustainability, there are nevertheless only a few who combine vegetarianism with wise ethical constraints, an attitude leading to fruition - in the real sense of the word, at that.

The twenty-nine main tenets of this religious community concern all areas of life, represent a global summary of moral and social conceptions and require actually nothing more and nothing less than an intense symbiosis with nature: Devotion to God, compassion with all living creatures and consequently a vegetarian way of life as well as a comprehensive protection of nature.

There are many requirements, such as the demand for respect between man and woman, reflection, contentment, tolerance as well as hygiene and purity rules. No idols exist; instead the admiration is dedicated to the living nature in its present animal form.

In the emergence of this new philosophy, the requirements for the protection of the desert's Flora and Fauna became popular and people grew rapidly devoted to them. Especially the respect for trees was quickly integrated into the everyday life: People became charitable towards and protective of them.

Researchers, fascinated by this remarkable philosophy, found out during numerous discussions and by careful observations that these centuries-old tenets even today still hold absolute importance for men, women and children likewise, and that consistently in theory as well as in practice.

Also priests and members of the "*nyati panch*", the community-instance monitoring adherence to the rules, acknowledged this scientific statement. So the result of an analysis of the official media of the Bishnois, the "*Jambh Jyoti*", cannot surprise when stating that almost all contributions were dedicated to the protection of animals and trees.

If a Bishnoi should be caught eating meat or causing pain to an animal, he is finished socially. In the small Bishnoi-villages it is almost impossible to escape the general attention and so aberrations become general knowledge fast. This fact strengthens the homogeneity of the group as far as questions of ecological ethics are concerned. Probably these ecologists managed their collective consideration towards nature in their barren homeland only with the help of insight and oversight and by that achieving their adherence to the rules that Jambeshwar had set out so long ago. And it is quite obvious that nature appreciates this respect!

A barren homeland

"All this talk about nature and wildlife protection would be more effective if each individual was to believe in the earth as a living, breathing entity and fight for its survival the way we do."

Johra Ram

The Bishnois can be found in the Hissar and Sirsa District of Haryana and in Abhor and Fazilka of the Punjab, in Uttar Pradesh, in Gujarat, in Madhya Pradesh, Delhi and Mumbai. But their concentration is in Rajasthan especially in the Districts of Jodphur, Nagaur, Bikaner, Barmer, Pali, Jalore and Sirohi. Rajasthan is one of the most thinly populated States with Jaipur as the capital. This Indian state is famous for idyllic and legally protected wild life reserves and infamous for the nuclear tests taking place there (1974 the first Indian nuclear weapon exploded in that area).

The weather conditions in that region can, with very good reason, be called extreme: Ninety per cent of the annual rainfall hits the ground during the monsoon period between July and August, temperatures in the hottest months of May and June reach 50 degrees Celsius and extremely violent dust storms can batter the meager countryside with 140-150 km/h.

A villager transporting water

Always recurring, typical motives on postcards, brochures, photos and travel descriptions are long camel caravans against the background of sharp edged dunes, riders with sunburned faces and multi-coloured turbans under a glaring sun - in short: the typical desert scene. But Rajasthan represents so much more. In that region a dynamic side-by-side of a hypnotizing colourful Yesterday can be discovered next to a stylish high-tech Today.

There are several local dialects in which people of Rajasthan converse, but Hindi and English are also spoken. The population lives predominantly in village communities of different density, in which as domesticated animals mainly cows, sheep and camels are being held. Customs, traditions, rituals and clothes are of impressive diversity and both Islam and Hinduism are practiced.

A variety of different plantations can be found, such as peanuts, soy beans, raps, flax seed, mustard, tobacco and cotton, but in this state also synthetic yarns, cement, television tubes, chemicals, fertilizers and electronic equipment are produced.

Even though the traffic routes are not yet very developed and relatively few roads and railways are available, it can nevertheless be stated that in this dynamic area there is plenty of room for the traditional and the modern which actually do co-exist in a most impressive manner.

Camel markets are important events in desert regions

The Thar Desert

"We never cut trees"

Suda

The area interesting us is situated in the northwest of India, i.e. the Thar-Desert, also called the Great Indian Desert. This region of life-hostile dreariness is covered with sand dunes and reaches over 200.000 km2 beyond the boundaries and into Pakistan.

Proof exists that about two thousand years ago this area must have been covered with thick rain forests. However, increasing population pressure and excessive felling reduced these forests and exposed complete hill slopes. Nowadays every one of us is aware of the climatic changes following such eradications, i.e. a gradual decrease in precipitations.

This combination sets the wheel of a vicious circle spinning when at a certain point in time tree roots cannot hold the centuries old soil any longer. Then just one strong rainfall is sufficient to wash away the earth of a complete mountain-slope and thereby not only exposing the area to gradual desertification but at the same time suffocating rivers and plains: A once fertile zone turns into a desert.

A typical Bishnoi village in the Thar desert: Huts in the middle of sand dunes with scarce vegetation

The Thar Desert actually is one of these forlorn places consisting of snakelike dunes that are broken up by plains and narrow naked hills, the so-called *bhakars*, which rise sharply from flat ground. As if they were alive, the dunes move incessantly and change into all forms and sizes - older formations on the other hand can freeze in a semi- or solid form and reach heights of about 150 meters. The vegetation consists of scrub jungles and the robust Khejri tree which is so undemanding that it manages to survive even in the most inhospitable areas.

However, apart from seeing sterile borders of arid wastelands, also an amazing discovery can be made: green belts among the monotonous and eye-fatiguing cloak of ochre! An impressive variety of durable plants presents living proof of nature's reverence towards the care and consideration of the descendants of Jambeshwar. So it becomes quite obvious that his centuries old and still valid guidance allows his followers even now to always find a modest but sufficient base of life - and that under the most difficult conditions.

When during cruel periods of droughts other inhabitants are affected in absolutely catastrophic ways, the Bishnois are not at all thrown off the tracks of their frugal routines. Even under such difficult circumstances they do not only manage to provide the necessary for themselves but are even able to uphold their care for animals and by that creating the particular little paradise that other parts of the world have not seen for a long time - or never at all.

Not only the protected rare Black Bucks and the delicate Chinkaras prosper here under human protection, but also herds of other animals and swarms of migratory birds flock to the Bishnoi villages knowing that in the proximity of these people they have nothing to fear. When witnessing how these wild creatures are so devoid of all fear that they even can be hand-fed, one is flabbergasted and wonders if these peaceful scenes actually take place on the same globe on which, without any questioning and by everyday routine, billions and billions of animals are fattened, abused and sacrificed on the altar of frenzy human consumption.

How in an extremely hostile environment was it possible for a society, for whom even the simple desert grass counts as one of their main resources and who again and again suffers from extreme water shortages, to create and maintain such an exemplary and heart-warming oasis of peace?

A Stable Desert Region

"Any change in the world has to begin within the society."

Johra Ram

So how do the Bishnois achieve to maintain this haven? A group of approximately hundred ecologists was also intrigued by that question when in 1988 they crossed the Thar Desert which was suffering from a period of extreme drought at the time. Their aim was to find out how this particular population achieves their remarkable immunity in times of crises that for others regularly lead to catastrophic consequences.

It seems that one of the most plausible explanations for this ability can be found in the Bishnois' wise and proven talent to manage rainfalls with extreme efficiency, to even collect dew drops from plants, to run a well functioning cistern system and, most of all, to prevent over-grazing by their domestic animals. This prudently organized system ensures sufficient water supply even under most difficult circumstances, for both humans and animals. Not only do the Bishnois share their scarce water resources with animals but they have also created additional reservoirs for them in their fields.

"Tanka" of a Bishnoi community near Peepasar: Rain is collected in a pit, which is covered with a lid and secured by padlock: water is very precious in the desert

Furthermore, there is normally no serious lack of food either, despite the extremely difficult environmental conditions: Millet is harvested, radishes, carrots, garlic and wheat, also sesame oil is produced. The cultivation methods are ingenious and perfectly adapted: the fields have been spread out intentionally over a large area in order to get the most profit from scarce and in time, place and intensity unforeseeable precipitations and by that increasing the chances of receiving at least here and there the necessary rain. Furthermore the collection of wild fruit and vegetables has long played an important role in the diet.

During drought periods in Rajasthan, the flames of one pyre next to the other could regularly be seen. These burning mountains, built with the carcasses of tens of thousands of buffaloes and other domestic animals having died of thirst, always had the consequences of forcing ruined farmers into ecological exile. So the experts are eagerly trying to find out why there never has been sight of such tragedies in the Bishnoi area, not even during the most difficult periods. Just the opposite - no horrific scenes but rather a modest and peaceful routine. Their singular affection towards animals, and a corresponding love for life in all its forms, has hitherto protected the Bishnois not only from disasters but also prevented them from becoming dependent on national assistance like others.

Should it be true that only the wisest survive? The Bishnoi example obviously affirms this question because even in dry periods they remain calm and stay in their villages. The precipitation may be missing but they have provided for this eventuality and find ways of optimally facing up to given conditions. In large underground tanks rain had been collected and during drought periods this reserve provides the necessary drinking water of which no drop is ever wasted. However, the water for the animals and washing must sometimes be brought in on camels' backs over long distances.

It is a well known fact that in desert regions the dry periods present immense problems. Some years ago Jodhpur was threatened by such a catastrophic drought that there was even talk of evacuating the overcrowded city. However, the problem could be solved by the completion of the Rajasthan-Canal and there is sufficient water available - for the moment.

A similar system was meant to make the surrounding rural areas less vulnerable. So water tanks were built in the villages and connected, by pipelines, to the city water supply. Indeed this seemed like a good idea at the time but unfortunately is not working. Whilst the system is still standing, the water supply is so scarce that in many villages this problem is the main topic during the long hot summer months. Sometimes the pipelines are completely dried up for long periods and on other days only a trickle of water filters through.

So the Bishnois had been well advised to take the question of a sufficient water supply into their own hands. The wisdom of the elders, who by the way are very honoured in this society, had also taught them not sell grain but to store a supply of three or four years worth in enormous containers, protected under cooling millet straw.

The visitor who has the pleasure of enjoying the hospitably of the Bishnois might be surprised by the pleasant coolness that the thatched roofs over the round huts provide even at 43 °C in the shade. When he talks to his hosts while dipping pieces of bread in white cheese and seasoning it with onions and pickled peppers, it is easy to forget being in a famine area. Trusting birds, flying in and out, support the impression of experiencing a touching desert idyll.

Cranes near a village where they are being fed every morning

These " Greens" do really manage nicely in their inhospitable homeland where during recent decades the milk sales proved to be an important source of income. Careful handling of resources thus not only provides sufficient food for humans and animals but also leads to prosperity: today it is not unusual that Bishnoi families deal in trucks and tractors, making good money. So it is not surprising that they belong to the most successful farmers of India.

But the milk production unfortunately leads to the problem of too many calves. Since cows, like humans, only produce milk for their new generations, the milk production is inevitably linked to births. Nevertheless, the problem is not quite as dramatic as it presents itself in countries of the European Union where farmers are paid by special premiums to kill the "waste by-product calf " as young as possible; in order to control the "meat-mountain".

The Bishnois never kill a calf. The male animals are used for work. However, should there be too many, they have to be sold, preferably to other Bishnois. But even if animals end up with outsiders they still stand a reasonable chance of dying a natural death. The life of cattle in India actually does enjoy higher value than in Europe or America. However, unfortunately, India is adapting more and more to Western conditions also in this regard.

In order to determine the effectiveness of traditional and modern methods in the context of fast changing environmental conditions, further research not only in the Bishnoi area is envisaged but also with their neighbours. One would like to find out how the Bishnois have managed steadfastly to pursue their active consideration for the environment and a vegetarian life-style over so many centuries: and that in an area where such values are not at all shared and where meat consumption and environmental degradation are increasing more and more (for example: in 1993 the Indian government finalized an anthropological investigation and came to the surprising result that 88% of the population consumes meat).

Even though the Bishnoi-people are presently still protected by their very own wisdom, a disturbing question remains open all the same: How will a fast spreading urbanization in all corners of the world eventually affect any hitherto religiously pursued ideology of sustainability? Are unique traditions going to be watered down in the future or even completely dissolved?

Fortunately it can be stated that regarding the Jains, about whom we talk in Chapter II, no such negative tendencies have been discovered - quite the opposite. And also the Bishnois, though absolutely going "with the times" (in the good and sometimes in the less good sense of the word), seem to continue their role as stewards and protectors of Flora and Fauna - with the usual determination and devotion, at that.

Bishnoi people in front of their huts

Getting Acquainted

"How can People Kill Animals for Supper?"

a Bishnoi child

The more one hears and reads about the Bishnoi people, the more the desire grows for an opportunity to learn from them. Even if a huge tourist industry is not in the interest of that rural population (which developed some distrust of tourists because of a series of very bad experiences), the earnings through the sale of different products are nevertheless very welcome.

There are several formulas for the discovery of the Thar Desert: by Jeep for the normal tourist- or even by camel safaris. However, the latter are only recommended for people in excellent health because the traveler will be exposed to a demanding and rough environment and has to cover 12-15 miles per day.

Preferably one should make one's way to the sandy home of one of the world's finest ecologists between October and March. During these months the weather is relatively cool and dry.

Trips are being organized by different travel agencies and usually start with a long flight to Delhi. After a comfortable pause, the journey continues towards the second biggest city in Rajasthan: Jodhpur. This town, near which many Bishnois are living, has a rough desert climate. It was founded in 1459, flourished to a center of commerce in the 16th century and is still well worth visiting today.

In the center of Jodhpur, enthroned on a rock with a height of about 120 meters, the gigantic Meherangarh Fort rises into the sky. This is one of the most impressive forts in India and at the same time, protected by an enormous wall, one of the largest in Rajasthan. The complex consists of luxury palaces with heavy doors which are a reminder of a more than lively military history (the main entrance still has traces of canon balls stemming from one of the many battles that were fought there) and impressive collections of paneling, sedan-chairs, miniature paintings, musical instruments, clothing, uniforms and weapons - all vivid souvenirs of Rajasthan's turbulent past.

It is quite obvious that in this city nobody is afraid of dazzling colours. Men in opalescent turbans in light green, pink, red and orange can be seen, with heavy gold earrings and unusual beards. The women wear predominantly clothes of a red colour; their skirts are normally decorated with small pieces of mirror. The lower arms are often completely covered by bracelets; furthermore they carry fancy and flamboyant ear- and nose-rings, which are connected by gold chains dangling on their cheeks.

When the visitor admires this vibrant and chaotic city chaos from the lofty height of the fort, he is liable to forget the breath taking heat and the desert sand between his teeth.

But from this high look-out some other sentinels are also interested in what is going on in the city: vicious looking Longbilled Vultures wait for their call of duty at natural garbage disposal units. They clean the carcass of a cow in less than half an hour and thereby make a commendable contribution to hygiene and public health in the crowded city.

If one decides on a longer stopover in this city of palaces and museums, an accommodation selection is available that suits all wallets. With sufficient funds, one can even take up "residence" in a restored maharaja-palace.

This temple in Mukam is devoted to the memory of Jambeshwar's death

When wandering through the narrow and winding streets one is liable to discover, in the vicinity of the town tower, a buzzing medieval bazaar for the purchase of souvenirs. Small shops offer almost everything, such as textiles, carpets, marble intarsia, mirror embroideries and classical silver jewelry. This area is also famous for antiques and their high-quality reproductions.

About 65km away from Jodhpur, one finds the old city Ossian that, in former times, was an important religious center and still houses Rajasthan's largest accumulation of early Jain and Hindu temples. In that area any interested tourist can discover the evolution of Indian temple architecture between the eight and the eleventh century. Especially the Surya- (sun) and the Sachiya Mata-temples are famous for their beauty. Accommodation is available in a camp, from which one can enjoy a beautiful view over the city.

Impressive even in this desert landscape is the obvious delight of the inhabitants for lively colours; as if they needed to make up for the depressing desert ochre by their own eye-beguiling choices, strengthening the impression of vitality and their enthusiasm for festivities. In that area there seems to be no room for boring events or pale shades!

Even though the Bishnoi areas are actually situated in the closer environment of Jodhpur, the route to them leads through seemingly endless and barren desert areas that show themselves in a diversity of pale browns. Even the sky appears pale in this colourlessness, which is livened only occasionally by some green dots of shrubs and trees. But, although Mother Nature appears to have been particularly unfair here, the Thar Desert is nevertheless the most densely populated desert area in the world! The secret of this flourishing in a hostile environment can only be explained by the pacific ways of its inhabitants.

When the driver points out to his guests the first emerging animals it is clear that one has almost reached the destination. The Bishnoi settlements must be near. And really! The desert-yellow is gradually being replaced by green vegetation and more and more herds of trusting animals can be discovered. They not only graze without any fear in the oases, but they amble also, as can soon be discovered, among the humans in their villages (hamlets). Also the many birds

Bishnois in the Lohawat temple, dressed in their typical white outfit

do not seem to have any fear (it is quite common that they even visit their human friends in their houses) and peacocks walk around everywhere without a care in the world.

In some villages the visitor might even be welcomed personally by the chief of the community and be invited to participate in the simple life for a while. If he is lucky he may observe a session of the "*Panchayat*" ceremony (the village jurisdiction under the presidency of five wise men) where heated arguments are prudently defused.

The Bishnois live in clean and airy thatched huts with separate cooking units and, sometimes, adjacent fenced-in pastures. In most of these villages there is neither electricity nor telephone and the only means of transportation are carts pulled by camels.

Life generally is relaxed and serene. Even if the surroundings show pitiless harshness, inside the villages the philosophy of Jambeshwar is translated into a warmhearted and dignified togetherness. Humans and animals live in peace, which not only brings blessings to the animals but also to the human protectors at the same time: the Bishnois enjoy a particularly good health.

Bishnois at the Mukam fair

The Bishnoi farmers keep camels, cattle, and buffalos, however none of these animals are slaughtered. But the milk for food and also the dung for burning and building material play important roles. Fallen branches are gathered for heating purposes, however, never are they "wasted" on the otherwise in India common burning of deceased. "We bury the dead and let the earth take back what it gave to us," explains Dev Ram from Guda Bishnoi and adds: "Cremating the dead requires wood. But Jambeshwar said that killing a live tree to get rid of a dead body is ridiculous." That is why the Bishnois bury their dead and do not even erect a headstone. There are specific grave-yards for this community.

Visitors are welcome on the condition that they respect the strict Bishnois' way of protecting nature. To ensure this, any newcomer will be observed carefully. However, after having been accepted as a friend, he may enjoy the smile of the people, their famous hospitality and participate also in their traditional meals, which consist of cooked vegetables, white cheese, buttermilk, spices, different breads and an impressive quantity of lentils.

Since the Bishnoi areas are scattered in the desert, overnight accommodation can be arranged but it is normal to visit these villages by day trips, which can start anywhere in Jodhpur or Bikaner, Nagaur, Phalodi, Osian, Barmer, Balotra or other places.

In the villages a variety of souvenirs is available, such as pottery articles, carpets (*dhurries*) from cotton, camel or goats hair, embroideries, hand woven textiles such as clothes, table cloths and blankets.

It can be noticed that, even in smaller places, there is no lack of know-how relating to crafts: The weavers, potters and shoemakers have learned their masterfully controlled art from their ancestors over generations and like to show them off proudly to their visitors, who may, when desired, also have a go on the potter's wheel or the loom.

Of course, there are also carpenters but they have to tackle a very special problem concerning their procurement of raw material: they have to wait patiently until the necessary wood has fallen down and is available for collection and processing.

The tall and slender men of the Bishnoi community are dressed in white (turbans, shirts and *dhotis*); this is the symbol of their steadfast belief and an outer sign of purity and restraint. Women on the other hand, the "symbol of creation", impress by vibrant colors such as red and orange skirts, with gold ornaments and massive gold jewelry in form of bracelets, rings in the left nostril and ankle chains. The jewelry around the neck and in the left nostril are very special for the Bishnoi women who can be recognized by such pieces.

The everyday life of these humans is still determined in all details by the tenets of the wise Jambeshwar: Cleanliness and careful hygiene protect against diseases, animal protection brings about the fertilizing of the soil and self-sufficiency prevents dependencies.

The Indian caste system has no grip in the Bishnoi philosophy, in which generally equal rights between the sexes also prevail. The right to vote is exercised with enthusiasm; in 1987 the first Bishnoi woman was elected into a parliament situated outside of her own municipality.

Perhaps one would like to organize the trip in such a way that one can mix with the many visitors at the important celebration to the memory of Jambeshwar; this event takes place annually in February/March in Mukam (Mukam meant: he lived here).

An interesting detail is worth mentioning because it is typical for this religious community: This Jambeshwar temple does contain accommodation for guests - and storage space for grain reserves which are donated by visitors for pigeons, peacocks and other animals. For the daily feeding sessions special places next to the temple have been created.

Everyone, regardless of race, nationality and faith, may visit this memorial and participate in the rituals, which are led by a Bishnoi priest.

There is also a second Jambeshwar festival, however, it is much smaller and visited mainly by local people who arrive with camels, trucks or also on foot. This event is more like an agricultural fair.

Furthermore, the cleaning of the Jambeshwar Lake is considered as a religious as well as a community service. The dug-up mud is carried to the surrounding mounds and by this method the conditions of the soil are being improved, slowly but steadily.

A Romance with Nature

"Animals are sacred "

Bana Ram

"The animals could identify the members of the Bishnoi community inhabiting the desert districts of Rajasthan by their white dress and even by their gait"

Harsh Vardhan in an article in the "Hindu" - October 1998

Some Black Bucks who can be seen frequently around Bishnoi villages

When all those years ago Jambeshwar wandered through the barren lands of Rajasthan, his teachings convinced his fellow men of the fact that nature is to be respected and defended by all means. These teachings remain true even today, because after all it was their observance, which eventually created a unique paradise. Certainly, everyone has, at one time or another, dreamt of such harmony where for wild animals the sight of humans does not automatically bring about an intense feeling of threat and the reflex to flee - just the opposite. Here they move freely and approach humans without hesitance. This confidence and a natural and somewhat unspectacular routine in the caring togetherness of man and animal flabbergasts visitors.

The Bishnois not only feed and water their animal-"children" but also supply them, if necessary, with hand fed medicines and bury them carefully at the end of their natural lifetimes.

It even occurs that Bishnoi women nurse orphaned or injured animals. The bonding is so astounding that M.K.Ranjitsinh in his book "Beyond The Tiger" published the photo of a young Bishnoi woman breastfeeding a fawn. So it is really not surprising that a maternal- and protection-instinct as strong as that makes women react with energy and powerful determination when discovering offenders.

It does seem that women have developed the strongest bond with animals. So an old folksong, dedicated to Demoiselle Cranes, goes: " Oh crane, my husband was now over one year away. You are my sister and have wings, bring a message to him... "

Well! The sister is a bird? There goes one evolution theory after the other out of the window because the Black Buck antelope (*Antelope cervicapra*) is also considered as son, the cattle as family members and the Khejri trees as holy men. For these humans every form of life in the desert is of importance and therefore enjoys the respect and the affection to which each family member is entitled.

In the life of these people a prominent role is played by the Black Buck - a robust animal with a darkish coat on his back, white belly and impressive curved horns. According to legend it was Jambeshwar himself who demanded that the Black Buck should be respected in his place and for that reason hunting this animal is an absolutely unforgivable sin.

In every discussion with a Bishnoi member, sooner or later, the phrase will be heard "*Kalo hiran to mharo babo se*" (the Black Buck is our revered animal). Even though ruthless parvenus like Khan kill them, these rare and vulnerable animals, which can easily die of fright and shock, are not only loved and admired by the Bishnois but also defended at actually all cost.

Not too long ago enormous herds of Black Bucks roamed through the northern and western plains of India but today not more than approximately 9,000 of these animals live in Rajasthan (no figures are available from other regions). Since unfortunately this species multiplies extremely slowly, it has now to be considered as seriously endangered.

Not only environmentalists worry about the potential disappearing of Black bucks but also the Bishnois fear the loss of their animal-symbol of prosperity which seems directly linked to their own well being. Thus one is not too surprised to learn that these non-human friends are permitted to graze on all fields. However, the damage is limited since they wander around and never remain too long in a particular place - this "system" allows individual farmers to control and handle their losses.

In this forlorn corner of the world the harmony between humans and nature is almost palpable and each erring cow can be sure to always find attention and food from whatever person it might turn to - if it is not even looked after along with the family animals.

All these anecdotes just add pieces to an unusual overall mosaic. The caring for all animals is nothing but a normal event in the everyday life of these "real animal people". A smaller yield for human consumption is accepted in the interest of four legged "gate crashers". One gives gladly. Farmer Bhuvani Ra is even convinced that the harvest becomes the more successful the more the animals eat.

"Black Bucks are the followers of Lord Krishna. It is a sin to kill them!" says Dasrathi Nayak from the Ramunda village where the largest concentration of Black Bucks can be found.

The fact that one can still see Black Bucks at all, today, in spite of massive and brutal hunting by yesterday's princes and today's poachers, is almost exclusively the merit of the Bishnoi communities. But despite all their efforts, this species still remains threatened and is disappearing slowly not only in India but also in Bangladesh and Nepal; it is already extinct in Pakistan. It is therefore in the areas of the Bishnois where the elegant male animals with the beautifully curved horns can best be observed when they roam in the company of their clear-coloured harems.

Without any doubt the concern for animal protection still remains one of the most important elements in the philosophy of these people. Although older Bishnois are moaning - like all other parents in the world - about education problems and the carelessness of their offspring, they nevertheless have to admit that it is their sons and daughters who confront hunters in the quickest and most determined fashion.

Also the pretty Indian Chinkara Gazelles (*Gazella gazella*), who with their elegant features and large eyes seem to have stepped out directly from the world of fairy tales and are the favoured hunting-victims of neighbour tribes, enjoy special attention. Unfortunately, despite all these efforts it has not yet been possible to prevent the shooting of hundreds of these animals by poachers - who do not even hesitate to murder humans trying to stop the massacre.

After yet another one of such dramatic events the population of the small city Meena ki Dhani, 70 km from Jodhpur, was in mourning because of the death of Ganga Ram who had been shot by poachers in the year 2000. This incident led to a more urgent demand to equip the Bishnois, who have done so much for nature, more effectively and by that enabling them to take the defense of nature into their own hands.

An Indian Gazelle

But even if for the followers of Jambeshwar the holiness of all creatures is recognized and respected, this consideration by no means stops with breathing beings but extends to all aspects of nature.

In the *Orans* (holy groves) not only animals are protected against damage but also the trees. One of these regions is Guda Bishnoi Khejarli, a nature reserve with the size of 13000 km2. And exactly in this holy place film star Khan had committed his poaching crime, which for the Bishnois represents a violation beyond any compare.

As was already mentioned earlier, the Khejri tree is a very special friend of the Bishnois and plays an important role not only in the every day life but also in the spiritual context - and that since the dawn of history. One speaks already of the Khejri in the Vedas, the Sanskrit Epos and in Indian desert folklore. No other tree is adored like that. This can certainly be explained to a large extent by its lucrative versatility: It is resistant, resilient, stores water by its deep roots, binds soil and stands for an important source of raw materials.

Today it is becoming clearer and clearer what the Bishnois discovered centuries ago and what our scientists only now publish as their latest wisdom: the indispensable value of trees for human life. Everywhere in the world desperate efforts are being made (and astronomical amounts of money invested) to repair the damages caused by deforestation. But chances of success remain doubtful and governments can but dream of the success of the Bishnois.

Chipko

"What do the forests bear?
Soil, water and pure air.
Soil, water and pure air.
Sustain the earth and all she bears."
Song of the Chipko women

"We must remember that the main role of the hill forests should be not to yield revenue, but to maintain a balance in the climatic conditions ...."

Sarla Behn in 1978

One smiles about the dreamy tree huggers! But considering that this New Age movement finds more and more followers, there must after all be some profit that the friends of trees get out of this particular activity?

Indeed, it has been stated that trees can heel, relieve stress and that their "stillness, strength and balance" makes people more relaxed, helps them to sleep better and to reach decisions more easily.

However, the positive strength of trees is not at all a discovery of our time. Already in the Rigveda (2,500 B.C.) one speaks about the fact that the blessings of trees and herbs can heal almost all threatening illnesses - from head to foot, from the normal headache to the serious heart attack.

The adoration for trees is very old and runs like a red thread through all cultures across the globe. "Holy" trees were the "*Manahil*" for the Arabs and "*Nemeton*" for the Romans. It was expected of Persian saints that they would plant trees, the Osmans spoke of the "tree of life" and in the Indian Bhagavad Gita the tree symbolizes the Universe. For the Druids nothing was holier than the oak, which in their philosophy represented the source of all spiritual wisdom.

Buddha experienced his enlightenment under a tree, which can still be seen today. He is also said to have made the following observation: "The tree is a peculiar organism of unlimited kindness and benevolence and makes no demand for its sustenance, and extends generously the products of its life activity. It affords protection to all beings, offering shade even to the axe men who destroy it"..

In this overall context, the Bishnois' admiration of trees is not particularly worth mentioning, however, a dedication leading to such extreme self sacrifices is not known in any other culture. For the Bishnois the memory of Amrita and her friends is still very much alive and led even in the year 1973 to a similar, although fortunately less tragic incident in the village Gopeshwar: workers employed by a sports article company wanted to take up felling in the surrounding forests.

Inhabitants of many local villages streamed in, cried "*Chipko! Chipko!*" and hugged the trees. They clung to the trees and held them with determination, not in the least being deterred by the axes behind them. The workmen fled in panic.

Even though this particular event luckily ended without any bloodshed, it nevertheless became the foundation of the famous resistance movement "*Chipko*". This pacific program fights deforestation, especially in the Indian Himalayas of Uttar Pradesh (Uttaranchal since 2001) and, of course, in the Bishnoi areas.

These zones are protected with great devotion by the local populations, who consider the creation of nature reserves and the planting of trees as an act blessed by God. Even if originally this nature-protection stems from religious or c ultural sources, the "by-product" is not only a remarkable richness in animal and plant life but also brings along efficient soil-protection and much needed water storage.

The *Chipko* women are aware of the importance of healthy forests and sing about them. They know how much of their tradition is intertwined with trees and that inconsiderate felling or a lack in diversity leads to inundations, erosion, droughts and climatic changes.

In acknowledgment of the importance of trees for a healthy ecological system and as respect for the Amrita-martyrs, who were only recently honoured by the Indian government as the first ecological heroes, an annual festival is organized, the Van Mahotsav. Furthermore in 1988 the village Khejarli was proclaimed a national monument.

The ancient Bishnoi theses, after which forests precede human civilization and deserts follow it, does not only attract more and more attention everywhere but has also led to the establishment of the convention to fight desertification. At the end of the year 2000, a Congress was held in Bonn in order to look for solutions regarding the emerging developing disasters. Although the reasons, i.e. over-grazing, clearing and destructive agricultural practices, are known and understood perfectly, an effective healing-process of environmental scars does not seem to have been initiated up to now.

All around the globe clearing has led to serious problems, for example in China. There, caused by high water consumption and uncontrolled clearing of forests, a wide soil erosion has advanced the Gobi desert a hundred kilometers near the center of Peking. Now strong sandstorms unload annually a million tons of sand over the city.

Also the inhabitants of Inner Mongolia were shocked, when in January 2001 they discovered thick yellow layers on the ground: whirled-up sand of the desert Gobi had mixed with snow and tainted it.

The situation in Africa is even more dramatic because a loss of land of approximately 100 square kilometers per day has been estimated. Intensive exploitation of the soil is given as the reason for this dramatic situation, which forces three million humans to look for new habitats every year.

Example Tanzania: Three hundred thousand people are living in the area of the Usambara mountains in the Northeast of the country. Only one hundred years ago the soil on the mountain-slopes was the most fertile for Flora and Fauna in all of East Africa. Now the majestic forests have disappeared. One tries to compensate by the introduction of gentler traditional cultivation methods, nursery gardens and the distribution of trees to farmers in the area.

Also in South America the tropical rain forest, which constitutes a sixth of the earth's surface and a habitat for half of all living species, is being destroyed with a breathtaking speed. Half of the forests were already ruined in the last century and if the actual destruction rate continues, nothing of earth's breathing lungs will be left in the mid 21st Century.

As a consequence of such brutal exploitation not only trees disappear but also healthy soil, more and more animal species and even human tribes living in the respective areas. These are driven to misery and following decadence so that old cultures and their wisdom are lost along with the decline of peoples.

It should not be forgotten that a quarter of all our medication contains plant-elements from the tropical rain forests: raw materials for medicines. Since only two per cent of all plants have up to now been tested regarding their effectiveness, we could ruin our chances of finding amongst the remaining 98 percent those cures, which are so desperately needed.

But what is the reason for those even quite often nationally subsidized destructions? Mainly cattle breeding! The appetite for ever more meat is so enormous that rain forest areas, the size of Europe, have already been destroyed in the search of satisfying it - and an end to this eradication is nowhere to be seen.

Even if some western nations profit from this situation more than others, the bill will eventually have to be footed by the entire world community - also by those who think they get away with keeping complete cattle herds just for the production of dog and cat food. Furthermore: burning forests contribute to a large extent to the destruction of the ozone layer, the dramatic consequences of which do not respect any boundaries!

It is assumed also that the floods in Arkansas and Ohio in the year 1997 are a direct result of the substantial felling which took place in the interest of the timber industry and large scale breeding of poultry and pigs.

Possibly US president Clinton had these problems in mind when he offered a special farewell gift to the American people before his departure: He created seven "national monuments" by preventing the exploitation of more than 4,000 square kilometers of federal real estate in Montana, California, Arizona, New Mexico, Idaho and on the Caribbean Islands.

"We think that our future and our country, air and water belong together and that we do not only have to protect our historical inheritance, but also our natural treasures", he said when making his announcement in the East Wing of the White House.

Previously Clinton had protected eleven areas by the limitation or interdiction of traffic and commercial exploitation, and enlarged already existing reservations, so that the total area amounts to now approximately 240,000 square kilometers.

When one considers that by its roots each tree holds water and at the same time breathes liquid back into the atmosphere, the wisdom and shrewdness of this special gift becomes clear - both droughts as well as floods are going to be prevented by it. Trees are the air conditioning system of our earth and deserve also serious respect in their role as weather stabilizers.

The Bishnois have been giving this appreciation for such a long time now. It is interesting that all the efforts of today's politicians, and recommendations of scientists, reinforce in an amazing way Jambeshwar's vision of so long ago: excessive clearing leads to famine. History has proved him right over and over again.

One can but wonder why people everywhere do not at least listen to his wise advice. Why do the members of the UNCCS, who are never afraid of attending far away conferences, not book a flight to Jodhpur instead and look in that particular area for solutions of problems which already have been resolved there.

There may be many religions demanding respect for nature but the Bishnoi members with their global and holistic understanding form an exception all the same. Even considering that nature did not present itself to them in its most attractive form and showed them instead of sumptuous green valleys and seas of blossoms just a dry, dusty and devastated face, the Bishnois nevertheless love and adore what they see and have made consistent conservationism the pivot of their own terrestrial life.

If we could translate our obviously fast and globally growing uneasiness into consistent nature protection, there might be reason for more hope. The time for a new ideology is here, along with a need for a different style of life: based on a desire for unity and not on economical development models.

The Bishnois have understood this truth for a long time already. Their conviction that each living being has the right of fulfillment, unimpaired in its individuality and spiritual destiny, can be an example to us all. There just is no better way into a peaceful future.

Bish-noi - twenty-nine

.....is the number of tenets representing the basis for the social life of the Bishnois. These old rules not only address spiritual aspects but offer, in a surprisingly enlightened way, guidance in human co-existence and regarding the relationship between humans and animals. Furthermore solid hygiene-precautions are addressed which have proven their value not only in the past but even today help keeping food under safe conditions in a difficult desert climate.

The most important element is the spiritual demand to turn to Vishnu, stipulating rules for prayers and meditation and certain periods of fasting.

The recommendations governing human communities claim first of all the respect between sexes, they demand composure, comprehension, honesty, forgiveness, contentment and warn against greed and anger and also against too much criticism - against oneself and others.

Coconut shells are being burnt during the annual fair in Jamba

Of special priority are the rules regarding the treatment of animals. Not only is meat absolutely forbidden but also an all embracing compassion with animals is a must. Animals are not to be killed, however small they might be. There are special and detailed instructions regarding husbandry, one example is that it is forbidden to castrate bulls. In an effort to prevent animals from harm, also food and fire-wood is to be inspected to ensure that all tiny hidden creatures can be saved.

Also the protection of trees is required. Since they may neither be felled nor the branches cut, dried dung and coconut shells are recommended for use on fires.

A large number of the rules address practical and beneficial routine-situations, like the requirement to wash daily, to filter milk and water. In this context the consumption of opium, tobacco and alcohol is forbidden.

29 Principles of Bishnoi Religion

1. Thirty days to be observed in seclusion after the delivery by a woman.
2. Five days to be observed in seclusion during the menses by a woman.
3. Taking daily bath early morning.
4. Maintaining calm and patience.
5. Maintaining cleanliness, inside and outside.
6. Taking meditation each morning and evening.
7. Worshipping Lord Vishnu every evening.
8. Always speak the truth.
9. Perform yajna daily.
10. Drink clean and filtered water.
11. Be soft while speaking.
12. Clean the fuel wood before it is used (no insects).
13. No theft to be committed.
14. Never abuse any one.
15. Never indulge in excessive arguments.
16. Observe fast on *Amavasya* (the day before no moonlight).
17. Piety and pardon to be maintained as way of life.
18. Always remember Lord Vishnu.

19. Be kind to living beings.
20. Crush greed, anger, lust and infatuation.
21. Do not accept even water from a non-Bishnoi (to maintain one's principles).
22. A bull not to be made bullock (to avoid cruelty).
23. No opium to be consumed.
24. Green trees not to be felled.
25. No tobacco to be consumed.
26. Cannabis not to be consumed.
27. No liquor to be consumed.
28. No meat to be consumed, and
29. Blue clothes not to be worn.

Excerpt from an article, "Bishnoi Society : Origin, Development and Present Status" by Bansi Lal Khichad in the Sangoshti Vaani (a journal), 9 September 1980, Year 3 Vol. 2 (page 7).

Comments by Harsh Vardhan

**

Bishnoi Fascination

This happened more than 25 years ago and is still alive in my memory:

After finishing the morning session of reporting a village gathering where the stiff collared bureaucracy was softening its steel-like hard approach to assist the uneducated peasants in the semi- arid district of Pali, I requested the Collector (top officer) if I could be offered a jeep to go into the countryside and find out for myself if I could spot some gazelles, for my train to Jaipur would depart only at about 9 pm. Having seen my hard work and genuine reporting, the Collector instantaneously gave me a driver with a jeep. Hari Ram, the photographer, joined me as we made forays into the scrub fields having no crop during the summer months. Gazelles were around the hamlets. They would run away when we tried to go nearer to have a close look for some photographs (no tele-lens in those days).

Our advances towards the beautiful doe-eyed animals alerted the villagers. They kept a constant vigil on our moves and also shouted at us! I was annoyed at the shouts and did not care for them and continued following the animals.

The deer ran towards a well populated village and through a village reservoir as we took the road to reach the point where the animals had gone. A group of people wielding batons stopped the vehicle abruptly. They almost challenged our entry and motive of chasing the deer. As an argument started, some of them searched the rear side of the jeep (any gun?). On being explained that he is a photographer and I a reporter; the local driver informing them in their dialect, a flicker of smile appeared on the faces of the people.

They understood our purpose. Gave us water to drink. And answered my volley of questions! The group was now totally friendly. Instead of replying to one of my questions, one youth asked me to go to his hut! I hesitated, why? "To answer to your question", he politely replied.

Inside the hut: a young woman in veil squatted in a corner. A young gazelle stood beside her. The man said a few words. The woman uncovered her breasts and started feeding the animal!

My eyes were opened: the mother of the gazelle had been poached a few days ago near the village before the villagers could capture those city folk; the young one was rescued, now being offered milk by a woman! A Bishnoi woman!

Stunned I stood with my head bowing down to the deeds of the Bishnois! My first encounter with the Bishnoi community! My first field experience with gazelles in the desert!

As shadows lengthened we returned to board the train. I slept to wake up again and again: the woman feeding the gazelle appeared in front of me in the compartment. She is around me even today; in thoughts at least!

I was enslaved by these people. Like I am today, knowing that many in this community have undergone changes in their life styles. Yet the tradition of saving the flora and fauna continues. In villages at least.

.....That was in 1975-76.

Peepasar

"Jathe hoiye nahi lilo baanth,

bathe pere nahi meri chhant."

(I do not cross the land where green trees are not present)

Jambheshwar

Peepasar (the birth place of Lord Jambheshwar) is to the Bishnois what Ayodhya (birth place of Lord Rama) is to the Indian communities (Hindus). This tiny village in Nagaur district of Rajasthan, where the seer was borne in 1452, has no mention on the maps one receives at bookstores all over India. It, however, has even today got indescribable inscriptions over the mental floppies of the Bishnoi community and stands as a mute testimony to what Jambeshwhar preached to people.

One of the 29 principles he enunciated was to conserve the vegetation in the desert and lead a life of sustainability in thinking as well as action. This was followed in letter and spirit by the people who faced recurrent drought conditions in the desert of India.

A tradition emerged from not touching a blade of vegetation in and around a place where a temple had been installed. Such a green reserve thus received religious connotations and was started being considered as "*Dev van*" (God's forest). In the desert, people call it "*Oran*" (for others, not for ourselves). Such "*Dev van*" or "*Oran*" (sacred groves) are seen to this day in numerous areas in India. They have crucial ecological influence in the socio-economic-religious firmament of village folk life.

Peepasar is located quite at the centre of the state of Rajasthan. This area is conspicuous for its extreme dryness and striking variations of temperature with highly variable rainfall. The relative humidity is low.

The village is dotted with sand dunes and the people live in clusters over an area of about 3.52 hectares. Sand dunes cover one-tenth of the land area. Of this, three-fifth is used for agriculture and two-fifth for pasture. Peepasar has four sacred groves which cover a total area of about 36 hectares.

A festival is organized every year around this temple in Peepasar reminding of Jambeshwar's birth in 1452

Uncertainties, related with excessive dependence on nature, have made conservation an essential habit for people of Peepasar. The water inputs are few but the commodity is well looked after and in a variety of ways:

Nadi: It is a natural depression where water is deposited during rainfall. Peepasar has 5 nadis which can contain sufficient water.

Tanka: It is a small though deep pit to store water for personal consumption. It is usually maintained near one's house. It can be rectangular or circular and is always closed from the top, having a lid with a lock to be put on. Its dimensions can be 5 ft x 5 ft x 10 ft. and bigger as well. Its capacity can be minimum 10,000 ltr.

Wells: It is dug manually. The depth of a well depends on the status of aquifer. The average diameter is 6 ft.

Tubewell: The tubewells are sunk differently, first a depression is dug manually, then a drilling machine is used. The Government sinks tube wells for greater augmentation of ground water for use by a village or several villages. Cash rich farmers also sink such tube wells in the desert region.

Handpumps: They are similar to tubewells though they are pumped manually. The Government provides them as service to village communities.

"Waste not, want not!" Peepasar people live by this philosophy. The wisdom of conserving water has been learnt through experiences with drought conditions. Utensils are cleaned with sand. Little water is used. Clothes are collected and washing is done weekly. People rinse hands in a dish after the food is eaten. During cooking, water is used in a minimal way.

Peepasar has about 30,000-35,000 trees. Barring a few eucalyptus trees, planted in recent decades, all other species are indigenous. Khejri (*Prosopis cineraria*) is the most prominent tree species representing 61% of total vegetation here. Bordi (*Zyzyphus mauritiana*) is next with about 13%, followed by Rohida (*Tecomella undulata*) which makes up 7.5%, and Ankara about 5% with Kumta (*Acacia senegal*) being about 4.5%.

Khejri is the life support system in the desert. The tree is used for its fruit pods called "*sangri*". Its leaves add vital inputs in the feed for cows and buffaloes. The tree can be used as fuel-wood as well. When it becomes old and dries up, the wood is used for the construction of sheds for animal, its pole for tying animals etc. The root of dry Khejri tree is used for building purposes as the root is considered stronger. The green Khejri always produces moisture. Hence, the tree is favoured in its green form in agricultural fields all over the desert, serving as a catalyst for the growth of plants around it.

Peepasar has four sacred groves :

Jamboji ki Oran(12.8 ha) - Within this sacred grove is located Jamboji's *saathri* (the place where Jamboji lived). People do not use the vegetation - adult and aging trees - in this sacred grove because they fear that they will face the wrath of the deity (Lord) if they fell these trees or exploit this vegetation.

If caught cutting a tree, the village committee can levy a penalty on the misconduct: plant 10 trees for every tree felled; donate grain for feeding birds, livestock and wild animals, and take a vow never to fell a tree again in an Oran.

There are about 200 trees in this grove. They are xerophytic and deciduous. The shrubs are succulent with very small leaves and no flowers. The ground vegetation is thick and bushy. The oldest tree, "*Doodhaji ka Khejra*", is said to be over 500 years old.

The Indian Gazelle is ubiquitous in this Oran. A desert fox, normally a nocturnal species, was observed during one mid-day in the region. Desert cats are also reported there. The bird species observed here include: Kestrel, White-backed Vulture, Grey Partridge, Common Peafowl, Red Wattled Lapwing, Blue Rock Pigeon, Indian Ring Dove, Rose Ringed Parakeet, Spotted Owlet, Green Bee Eater, Indian Roller, Grey Shrike, Black Drongo, Brahmini Mynah, House Crow, Redvented Bulbul, Large Grey Babbler, Indian Robin, Yellow Wagtail, House Sparrow, Tailor Bird etc. The Bishnoi committee organises an annual fair at this Oran dedicated to Jambeshwar.

Peepenji ki Oran(4.8 ha) - This sacred grove is located over a sand dune. It is surrounded from all sides by agricultural fields, and is like a well-wooded island of 4.8 ha. It is associated with a saint called Peepenji. This Oran is a common property of the villagers. Unfortunately only 9 Khejri trees are left here.

Hanumanji ki Oran(2.08 ha) - This grove is associated with Lord Hanuman and a small temple-like structure exists there with an idol of this deity. There are barely 5 trees left on this grove.

Maharaj ki Oran(17.12 ha) - This grove is at a distance of 3 kilometers from Jamboji ki Oran. It looks like a depression amidst sand dunes. It is meant for the care-taker for the Bishnoi *saathri* so that he can draw resources from the cluster of groves and not exploit the Jamboji ki Oran where he is supposed to live to maintain the *saathri*. There are 155 trees on this Oran.

There is one more (personal) Oran, a tiny one, within the holding of a resident, Mohan Singh, which is dedicated to his late father.

Each Oran of Peepasar has had varied experiences about biotic interference. While the Hanumanji ki Oran is the worst affected due to use by villagers, the other three groves appear to be seemingly well conserved.

The definition of sacred is anything 'made holy by religious association; exclusively dedicated; sacrosanct inviolable.' D. Brandis (1897), first Inspector General of Forest of India, defined that sacred groves 'as a rule are not touched by the axe, except when wood is wanted for repair of religious buildings'.

The sacred groves, therefore, ARE sacred. However, for certain uses by local people, they are being exploited to a small extent: for grazing, collection of leaves, twigs etc. - but not for felling down the native vegetation. Fruit pods of Khejri are collected. Shrubs and herbs are utilised for medicinal purposes. Wood is also collected (not obtained by axing a tree) for fuel-wood purposes. The fruits of Bordi (*Zyzyphus*) are eaten as vital nutrients. Leaves of trees, shrubs and herbs are utilized for grazing animals. Moisture from the trees is naturally utilised.

That is bio-diversity and conservation in the Indian countryside, a grass root conservation strategy in practice to this day: The diversity of species assists communities to resist or recover from environmental disturbances and long term climatic changes; every nation's bio-diversity is critical to its own sustainable development.

Peepasar village sustains on its local resources, met from agriculture fields and partially from such groves. The excess production in a grove remains there and adds to the cycle of natural reproduction. The community is understanding that the grove is sacred, thereby its vegetation is not to be exploited, serves as the guiding factor and one's additional demand is fulfilled only through the bio-resources of one's personal means.

The richer the Oran, the better needs are being fulfilled. This is how a village like Peepasar survives since time immemorial.

An example : Jamboji ki Oran meets 18% of grazing needs, 0.7% of fuel-wood requirement, 0.2% of pods of Khejri, and 0.1% fruits of Bordi - for local residents. Compared to this, the other three groves of Peepasar contribute much less. Jamboji's Oran has the biggest moral demonstrative value: we maintain our vegetation by way of conserving the sacred grove, and we sustain better and longer.

Peepasar has a population of about 2,500 people; the common religion of the people here is Hinduism. Not a single Bishnoi lives presently in Peepasar. What an irony! The birthplace of Lord Jambheshwar, founder of the Bishnoi community and religion, is devoid of Bishnois! The tenets of the Lord, however, are still respected even though his followers may not actually be residing in Peepasar any more. The ecological spirit is to be felt, to be assessed, and to be admired.

Dutybound We Live

All these many years ago, Jambeshwar would have hardly visualised that his teachings would live on to an extent that people give away their lives for wild deer or trees even in our age dominated by consumerism and materialism.

Researching the largely non-descript history of Bishnoi people, I came across Hanuman Singh Bishnoi in Jaipur. He edited a Bishnoi journal "Sangoshti Vaani", a vehicle of support for nature conservation. It listed numerous incidents of the brave Bishnoi rural folk who challenged poachers and nabbed many of them. An excerpt of this journal is given here:

19 January 1979: 5 persons of Kodu village in Badnawa Panchayat in Pachpadra tehsil in Barmer district, gunned down gazelles in a Bishnoi field in Rewanda village. Manohar Lal caught one of them, Karni Dan. He was beaten up until he confessed and vowed not to indulge in such a crime ever again in his life.

January 1979: Luna Ram Bishnoi saved a gazelle in Lakhasar village near Pilibanga in Sri Ganganagar district. He was intimidated by poachers. In turn he remarked : "...by the time I shall get killed at your hands, hundreds of other Bishnois would have collected here to give you the befitting lesson!" The injured gazelle was brought to the village and the poachers were made to apologise. A cash fine of Rs 501 was imposed on them which they readily paid.

21 January 1979: Parma Ram Bavri killed a gazelle in Phaglu Ram Bishnoi's agriculture field in Khara village near Phalodi in Jodhpur district. The poacher fled with the body by the time the Bishnois gathered to catch him.

22 February 1979: Prema Ram Bishnoi, a student, chased Kevla Ram Bhil taking away with him a poached gazelle in Thathia village near Shergarh in Jodhpur district. The body was retrieved though the poachers fled. A post-mortem was performed at Lohawat by Ridmal Ram, a teacher who was assisted by the Dechu police station.

1 March 1979: Mahendra Khan was caught by people while firing at gazelles in Chotina village in Jodhpur district. Faced with

the wrath of people, Khan vowed not to commit such an act again. He was fined Rs 45 which he paid to the village.

3 April 1979: Chatura Ram, Khema Ram and Trilok Ram were identified as the poachers having killed a gazelle near the hut of Bhiya Ram Bishnoi. A report was lodged with the police in Bap on 4 April and a post-mortem was performed the same day. One person was arrested and his gun secured.

8 April 1979: Chena Ram and others succeeded in recovering the body of a gazelle being whisked away by some poachers near Pilwa village in Jodhpur district. They could, however, not catch the culprits. The report was lodged with the Lohawat police station.

14 April 1979: Two gazelles were shot dead at Kasvo ki Dhani in Bhikamkhor near Osian in the Jodhpur district. No arrest was made.

3 May 1979: Dhana Ram Khichad retrieved a gazelle poached by Lakshmi Singh in Pilwa village in Jodhpur district. A report was lodged with the Lohawat police station.

20 May 1979: 2 gazelles were bagged in Kajala village in Hissar in Haryana. People demanded an arrest of the poachers. No action followed.

25 May 1979: Some Bavaris shot dead gazelles near Malsingh ki Sidh village near Jamba in Jodhpur district. A report was lodged with the Lohawat police station. The post-mortem was performed in Phalodi. One person was arrested on 27 May.

4 July 1979: Chena Ram Bhil shot dead a gazelle in Godara ki Dhani. Ram Lal, Phaglu Ram and Manohar chased them but could not succeed. The report was lodged with Lohawat police station.

13 July 1979: Babu Khan and Shaukeen Khan fired at gazelles at Kachhwanio ki Dhani near Bishnoiyo ki Dhani in Jodhpur district. People surrounded them as Jora Ram and Kishna Ram brought them to the village platform. The poachers were released after they paid the fine of Rs 600 and took the oath not to fire at wild animals again in their life. The gazelle was buried near the village. The money recovered was utilised to construct a memorial-platform for the killed animal.

21 July 1979: Nar Singh, the poacher, was caught near Gudha Bishnoiya in Jodhpur district. His accomplices fled away. He was

arrested after the Bishnoi people handed him over to the police station. The dead gazelle was given a ceremonial burial. Durga Ram, Bhanwar Lal Khawa, and Pokar Ram Siyag led the chase to bring the culprits to books.

27 July 1979: 7 persons poached a gazelle in Pali village in the Jodhpur district. Manohar Bhadu, Mangla Ram, Pukha Ram, Tulchha Ram and others succeeded in snatching the body as poachers ran away. Mala Ram Bishnoi, Sarpanch of Lohawat, lodged a report with the police. No arrest was made.

16 August 1979: A female gazelle was poached between Ketu Kala and Bhalu Kala villages near Shergarh in Jodhpur district. One person was caught in a chase while fleeing away in a chase made by Buddha Ram and Sukkha Ram. The poacher was handed over to the police.

25 August 1979: Poachers fired in the air as Birma Ram Baniyal chased them and identified the running persons. Some Bishnois guarded the dead body of the gazelle while others pressurised the poachers in an adjoining village to kneel down. The poachers reported the following day with an apology and took a vow not to hunt again. They were pardoned in a meeting attended by the entire village folk as the animal was given a burial.

8 September 1979: Nearly 100 Bishnois gathered to catch a poacher in Chotina village near Phalodi in Jodhpur district. The body of the gazelle was recovered. The poacher was fined Rs 601.

7 October 1979: A gazelle got killed in a road accident by a bus driven by Akbar, who put the animal in the bus hoping to carry it home. Kishan Lal Bishnoi, a passenger in the same bus, objected to his design. The angry bus driver pushed Kishan Lal out of the bus and drew off to nullify the opponent and also fulfil his objective. Kishan Lal hitch-hiked to Jodhpur (the bus was going from Barmer to Jaipur), gathered fellow Bishnois and swooped on the driver at Jodhpur bus station. The driver was made to apologise and the body given a burial.

9 September 1979: Chaina Ram received bullet injuries as he chased two Bhils trying to take away a poached gazelle in Dabli village in the Jodhpur district. A case was registered with the police.

29 September 1979: Vishna Ram Paliwal chased a poacher and caught him in Cherai village in Jodhpur district. He was fined Rs 102.

In Ghantiali village (near Phalodi in Jodhpur district), Bagdu Ram Bishnoi of Bhojasar and Multa Ram Bishnoi of Pilwa caught another poacher. He was fined Rs 51 and was released only after he knelt down vowing not to poach again in his life.

25 October 1979: A poacher was made to pay Rs 511 and made to vow not to hunt again in his life in Matoda village near Osian in Jodhpur district.

26 November 1979: Ram Niwas Bishnoi caught Dara Singh poaching a hare at Bakra Road in Jalore district.

2 December 1979: A poacher was caught by Bishnoi people in the Kanwalisa village in Nagaur and handed over to the police.

6 January 1980: A poacher was caught in Cherai in the Jodhpur district. He sought pardon. People did not accept it and handed him over to the police.

10 January 1980: An ex army personnel, Chunni lal, was caught by Prithvi Raj Beniwal and Bhadar Ram in Dulpura village in Sardulshahar village in Sri Ganganagar district. He was released only after he sought pardon and promised not to poach again in his life.

14 January 1980: A poacher was arrested in Rajod and Butali areas of Nagaur district in Rajasthan. The gazelle was recovered from his possession and was given a formal burial.

26 January 1980: Balwant Singh and Pappu were held shooting gazelles in Denewala village in Firozpur district in Punjab. People succeeded to catch them and tried to hand them over to the police. But the poachers sought pardon and agreed to deposit 50 quintal wheat for birds and gazelles. They were freed at this social punishment.

16 February 1980: Multana Ram Jangu and Haru Ram Jangu overcame a Bhil in Sanwareej village near Phalodi. He was fined Rs 2,100. The seized gazelle was buried near the Panchayat office.

27 February 1980: Bhuru Ram Bavri could not be arrested as he poached a gazelle in Kana Ram's field in Bhundel village in the Nagaur district in Rajasthan.

17 September 1980: Udai Singh, Ganga Singh and Mahipal poached a female gazelle near Bhatwadi Nadi in Rotu village in Nagaur district. Ramjas, Bhiya Ram, Mukna Ram, Ram Karan, and Dhanna Ram challenged them and did not allow the gazelle's body to be taken away. A report was lodged with the police station in Jayal.

20 September 1980: Some Bhils poached a gazelle in Bhatip village in Sanchore tehsil in the Jalore district. The case was lodged with the Raniwara police station.

28 April 1981: Some people, suspected as employees of the Excise Department, were observed firing at gazelles in Roda village near Nokha in Bikaner district. When chased by villagers they drove away.

3 August 1981: Hazari Ram Bishnoi chased away poachers and did not allow them to take away the dead body of a gazelle in Janglu village near Nokha in Bikaner district.

5 August 1981: People recovered meat (of gazelles) being sold at a shop at Bavghata near Agatalia village in Jodhpur district. Chunni and Luna Ram Bhil were arrested by the police.

12 November 1981: As news of a gazelle having been poached reached, nearly 60 Bishnois assembled at Sadri Tanka in Pilwa area in Jodhpur district. They could not catch any poacher. A case was registered with the Lohawat police station.

**

I have visited Hanuman Singh Bishnoi in his village in Phalodi tehsil in the Jodhpur district. There is no road. Camel cart and camel are used to reach through undulating sand dunes. About twenty five huts are huddled together over a brown porous sand surface, dotted by xerophytic trees and shrubs. Other huts are scattered far away.

We settle in a '*jhonpa*' (circular hut); it is quite cool, as though air-conditioned, compared to the heat outside. A crowd of local Bishnois and non-Bishnoi people gather, talk and share their experiences. We listen to the Bishnois and their knowledge which is not only down to earth but at the same time a real survival-success-package.

Hanuman Singh Bishnoi, his wife and some young family members

We think we know so much more than these rural people through our university education and visits to different Western countries. But the villagers demonstrate us their the values of life which sprout from the earth that here it is parched sand, wanting water for years.

Innocent faces gaze at us. The people desire to know who we are, what is our objective to be in their village, what do we do in life.....? Many of them have not seen a railway train. Their world extends from this village to that village. They have a strong bond with time and traditions. Time flies away. Tradition lasts longer. The tradition to give away life. One's life. For a wild gazelle......!

Aghast we listen from Hanuman Singh Bishnoi about the four '*sakas*' (sacrifices) of the Bishnois. Each is a bigger memorial than the other. Memorial for life to sustain life. Civilized or wild......

Harsh Vardhan....

.....is a very well known journalist and columnist who has for a long time already written for the most important Indian newspapers. His articles cover a variety of subjects because he is not only very familiar with the Bishnoi people but also a specialist in conservation. Because nature is so very important to him, he has over the years initiated a variety of projects which resulted in better protection of wildlife.

Harsh is a much sought after speaker who talks all over the world and with in-depth knowledge about the dangers facing our environment. He has worked with the WWF (as its Honorary Secretary for Rajasthan State) and is the presently Honorary Secretary TWSI (Tourism & Wildlife Society of India).

Needless to say that Harsh and his family never eat meat.

Chapter II

The Jains

'There is nothing so small and subtle as the atom, nor any element so vast as space. Similarly, there is no quality of soul more subtle than non-violence and no virtue of spirit greater than reverence for life.' **Mahavira**

This statue of 2.5 meter can be found in a cave near Ellora. "Parshvanath on the hill" from the year 1234

The endings of a rainbow?

Bhiki has her hair cut by the most expensive coiffeur in New York. In the south Indian city Sravanabelagola a young woman sits down on the ground on the eve of her new spiritual life, meditates and then lets her long hair be pulled out by an hours' long and very painful procedure.

Bharat has his clothes made-to-measure in London. When wandering from one dusty village to another, the nun carries nothing but a piece of white material around her body.

Vijay treats the carefully trimmed pedigree dogs of jet set members and, of course, is paid a handsome fee for it. Dhanwant works without any salary in a hospital for abandoned animals.

In his luxury mansion in Antwerp, Rahul treats his guests to a sumptuous meal, served for them on a table decorated with gold leaves. The only food of the day that the "sky-clad" (i.e. naked) monk receives from the inhabitants of an Indian village, prevents him from going to sleep hungry.

Can contrasts be more extreme?

.........On one side, the rich Indian family clans of diamond dealers with addresses in Tel Aviv, Antwerp, Mumbai, London and New York, who today handle almost fifty per cent of all raw diamonds. This line of business started its breath-taking success story some decades ago in Palanpur, which is part of the oldest Muslim state in India. In the beginning, the Jains, belonging to a minority, worked only as administrators or salesmen but, by a combination of intelligence and alertness, plus a sharp instinct for business, knowledge of human nature and the readiness to work also the smallest stones (that by others were considered as not worth-while), managed to introduce themselves little by little into the diamond market.

Today the Jain clans occupy a worldwide and very prominent role in this particularly complicated line of business; the largest company employing approximately 25,000 people.

.....On the other side of the spectrum are the Digambara monks who consider their extreme renunciation as an undeniable source for "exquisite feelings of happiness " and who, wandering around naked, disseminate their teachings, as others before them have done for such a long time already: Historians reported that in the Indian city Taxila (now in Pakistan), Alexander the Great had once discovered some naked men who sat in silent and deep meditation on the ground. These naked persons were only ready for a discussion with the young general after he had taken off his armaments and sat in the sand with them. Legend has it that this incident made Alexander terminate his conquest and return to Greece... These impressive Yogis must have been Jains.

Incompatible endings of the rainbow? Yes, so it might seem! But the first impression is deceptive! Because all these people, from whatever glittering or sandy everyday life style and from which ever different social layers they may originate, wherever they have chosen to live and with which intensity they adhere to their faith: they all are Jains following a common idea of overwhelming importance: *Ahimsa* = non-violence!

Bhattaraka from Melsittamur with guests from Gingee

The Common Path

Wise men have set up the doctrine of non-violence - for all!

For "all": Here we are not talking about just an insignificant community but about a philosophy to which some ten million Jains adhere worldwide. In India one finds them mainly in Maharashthra, Madhya Pradesh, Karnataka, Gujarat, Rajasthan, Uttar Pradesh and Delhi, but also in other states of India. The main centers outside India are situated in America and Great Britain. And all these followers are vegetarians (although not everyone is obliged to carefully inspect his food with his fingers to make sure that it is free of small creatures, before putting it in the mouth).

Their faith does not allow any exploitation of animals. Thus they are not participating in enterprises that use living beings as their "means of production". Instead the Jains are concentrating on other business sections and occupations, such as doctors (who will not prescribe drugs derived from animals), publishers, judges, lawyers, scientists, environmental oriented engineers, teachers, accountants and politicians.

It must be said that they are extremely successful in their self-chosen business environments. They are hard working and clever! They know what they want! They have influence! They are wealthy!

Generally speaking, the Jain-community belongs to the relatively wealthy middle class - without any illiterates amongst them. But even if the *Nabobs* in the community have achieved their prestigious status in the clothes- or jewelry-trades, they would never deal in skins, ivory, products made from bones or similar items.

What an impressive proof of the fact that consideration for non-human creatures does not necessarily have to bring about pale, out-of-touch dreamers or hippies not fit for reality. The Jains show their fellow men that a careful and considerate attitude does not end in an offside trap but can, just the opposite, lead directly to the frontline of the economic and financial world.

So it is not surprising that under such a combination of spirituality, world-openness and a routine full of life-wisdom, even the transition of a rich young man into a monk can turn into a Hollywood-like-happening: The magnificently dressed future monk is carried during the religious ceremony on the eve of his inauguration on elephant-back, accepting the applause of proud relatives, thousands of friends and well wishers, who in groups and clans had been flown in by charter planes. It goes without saying that at such occasions attendees and guests will be taken care of and looked after in a most impressive manner!

Even admitting that such a fairy-tale celebration presents a not too discrete show of money, prestige and power, it does, however, underline at the same time the particular conviction of all Jains, regardless of their social backgrounds, in view to their culture and tradition. Events like these confirm again and again that all members of this large community will, albeit from extremely different backgrounds, barefoot or on the back of magnificently decorated pachyderms, march vigorously towards the same goal - the elimination of *karma*.

The Jains' understanding states that the conscience of a person can only be as good as his deeds, and so the follower has guidelines in the form of a variety of techniques at this disposal. A rich pantheon of tenets and ethical requirements are the basis of daily religious practices, such as the acceptance of the solidarity of all souls, compassion and sensitivity, tolerance and forgiveness, self criticism and restraint, charity and an all-encompassing friendliness, truthfulness, integrity and respect for the right of others, plus frequent fasting and daily meditation, pilgrimages and sharing with guests.

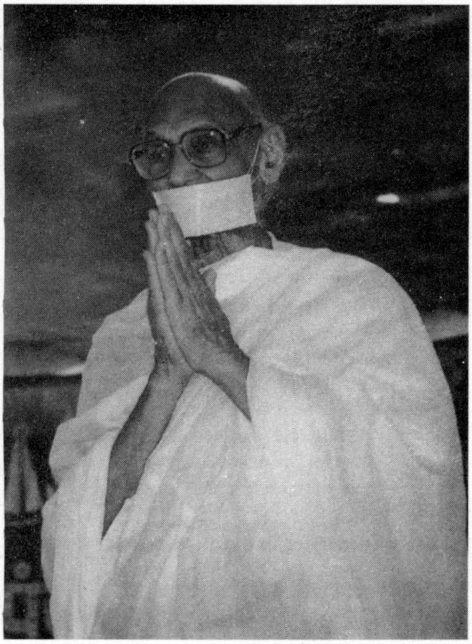

Admitting that even for a conscientious Jain lay person it is by no means a simple task to obey all vows and requirements, the rules for monks and nuns can only be described as standing for an extreme asceticism. They lead their lives under severe restrictions, which amongst others demands careful walking and carrying a cloth over the mouth by which even the smallest of animals are to be protected from harm.

All these different efforts, however, serve the same objective, which is *Nirvana* or *Moksha*. This means the release from rebirth, sickness, misery and death - and eternal bliss.

A Religion of High Ideals

Ahimsa is the Highest Truth

At no moment may a Jain lose sight of his personal strive for the alleviation of suffering. However, it is not sufficient either to lead one's own life according to these commands, it is also requested to prevent others from negative deeds, as far as at all possible.

Since the holiness of all life represents the basis of the Jain faith, no damage to any creature may be accepted, whoever commits it. This command holds true still today as it did, in the same seriousness, some millenniums ago. Already Mahavira preached of "a congregation of people and all other animals."

The Jainism is one of the earliest religions of the world. Scientists estimate the age of this philosophy at 2,500 years, which at the same time turns its followers into the first vegetarian community of the world.

No God is worshipped but the reverence is directed towards the twenty-four sages (*Tirthankara*): human teachers, who could even in earthly form attain the largest wisdom and the highest insight. Mahavira (599-527 B.C.) was the last of them. Born as a prince, he later spent twelve years in deep silence and in meditation, in order to still his desires and longings. He fasted during long periods and carefully avoided to harm any living creature whereby he, of course, included not only animals but also plants.

This sage created the Jainism by also using the theories of his predecessors. And it was also he who at the age of thirty years renounced all possession, including his clothes, and from that moment on went naked on his wanderings - and that for some decades to come. By his sermons he taught the importance of a positive attitude in life, preached of universal love and underlined that all living creatures, regardless of size, form or level of spiritual development, are equal and have a right to love and respect.

His teachings still are the basis for his followers and show wisdom, circumspection and are proof of an outright prophetic gift. How else could his recommendations point directly at the problematic situation that we are facing today? How else could he have known of the frightening ecological crisis of our times? Or are relevant reminders such as the statement "One who neglects or disregards the existence of earth, air, fire, water and vegetation disregards his own existence which is entwined with them" nothing but an amazing coincidence?

Of course, even a large community like the Jains cannot hold the flow of all misery and unfairness prevailing in this world. Furthermore are they not in a position to stop the massacre of a virtually astronomical number of slaughter animals everywhere and at all hours of the day. Thus they concentrate their efforts to alleviate suffering and at the same time are looking for ways of righting the wrongs. A thorough analysis of the damage caused by humans assists them in this task that they feel having been entrusted with.

Bahubali of Shravanabelagola, also known as Gommata and Gommateshvara. With a height of almost 18 meters is the highest monolith on earth. It symbolizes the Jain ideals of Ahimsa and was built at the end of the 10th century

Eternal Life, New Forms

In the opinion of the Jains all humans carry divine potential, which, by obeying the theories of the sages, by purification and discipline, can lead to the true and eternal determination of each individual. However, each soul is subject to its specific *karma*, which also determines the form in which it is born again at any given time.

The lowest form of beings, such as trees and vegetation, possess only the first of the five senses (touch, taste, smell, seeing and hearing), however, they are also capable of experiencing joy and pain.

Mahavira said that only the person capable of sensing the sacrilege and damage done to plants, is capable of the necessary respect towards nature. So it comes as no surprise that also the felling of living trees is strictly forbidden. Even metals and stones are to be treated with consideration because they also might have life in them.

These simpler organisms are followed by micro organisms and smaller animals with two (oysters and earth worms), three (millipedes and leave worms) and four (bees and flies) senses.

The highest developed creatures are animals - and humans, who possess also reason and intuition and who are therefore entrusted with an enormous moral responsibility, not only towards their equals but at the same time also regarding their relationship with the rest of the universe: eternal interaction will never allow humans to escape the ethical obligations that have been placed upon them.

Naturally, a philosophy like that contains a strong emphatic request for charity but at the same time this way of thinking can be considered as the cradle of all environmental protection and harmony with nature. In this context even the smallest of wrongs represents a serious offence.

In order to protect the soul of harmful acts and to purify it of negative thoughts, everyone is required to play an active role in the daily task of shaping of the world. The strength for this lies, according to the philosophy of the Jains, in each and any one of us humans who, so it is thought, represents an island of consciousness in an ocean of impetuously pulsating evolution.

They are wealthy. They give generously. They look after others.

"You are what you think!"

What better way to help improving our earthly home is there than active charity? That is why this community gives much of its accumulated wealth back to the community. In this context an amazing fact should be mentioned: One estimates that the Jains, who stand for not even one per cent of the Indian population, pay up to 50 per cent of all social expenditures! Additionally the relative criminality rate of this particular group remains by far below that of other parts of the population - in short: This minority is not only respected but also enjoys considerable influence in the country.

So in their quest of helping others, Jains created many schools, colleges, hospitals, social accommodations, lodgings, orphanages and emergency- and rehabilitation centres for handicapped, old, sick and poor people.

Jain Medical Institute-free health care for all

But not only humans are of importance. What better example for the concern of animals can be found than the bird hospital in Delhi, which is situated directly within the Jain temple opposite the historical Red Fort and which, representative of similar institutions of this religious community, will be described in a little more detail:

It all started in the year 1929 when only one physician was looking after the animals, and until 1946 the "hospital" consisted still of one single room only. However, today, because of never ending efforts and consistent commitment, this protection organisation stretches over a three floor building that offers room for grain stocks, conference and quarantine areas, wards with hundreds of patients that twitter in small or large cages, accommodations for physicians and a pharmacy. In a separate orthopaedic department animals with broken bones are treated; they receive plaster casts as well as physiotherapy.

Fledglings are being kept separately; they are under constant observation and hand-fed three to four times daily. New arrivals have to go into quarantine; a thorough medical examination follows to determine the adequate treatment in order to eventually be able to heal them.

Consulting periods of 12 hours are held seven days per week but, even at night, the person in charge is capable of providing first aid and looking after the birds until they can be examined the next day by the on-duty physician.

Dharamsthala. The Annapoorna dining hall can accommodate three thousand guests. Annapoorna is the name of the Hindu goddess of food. In the tradition of generous hospitality, each pilgrim is a welcome guest. Regardless of caste, birth and tradition free food and accommodation is offered to all

According to statistics, about 30,000 birds of all kinds are treated annually as in-patients and another 10,000 that their owners bring in just for examination and therapy-advice. New arrivals are at a record height during the hot months when compassionate people are taking many birds suffering from dehydration to the emergency unit.

The patients are looked after carefully and with dedication - and absolutely free of charge. There are no official subsidies and the complete set-up is based exclusively on donations. A great number and variety of loyal individuals meet the obviously enormous need for financial resources in a most reliable way.

Not only in the capital but also in the whole of the country and wider world are such achievements, based on effective altruism, greatly admired. This marvellous organisation stands for and demonstrates the blessings that can be brought about by the determination and goodwill of many different people from the most diverse social backgrounds and income brackets: the Jains!

The terrace of the Bahubali temple and the Bahubali statue of 8.5 meters. These buildings, situated 20 kilometers East of Kolhapur in Maharashtra, are used mainly for educational purposes and are open to members of all religions and castes

Live and Let Live!

"The Philosophy of non-violence is pure, unchangeable and eternal"

The sages said that, at a certain level, prosperity becomes superfluous and even damaging. So the extremely wealthy diamond dealers might be, and with reason, pleased about their professional achievements but they are just as proud regarding their charity. The Antwerp Jains showed their generosity in an especially impressive way when after the Indian earthquake in 2001 they transferred donations of record amounts into their devastated homeland.

In the court of Sharavanabelagola Mangayi Basti two brahmacharis of the local spiritual school (Gurukula) and children are singing a hymn to praise Bahubali

In a world of increasing greed and subsequent rampant ruthlessness, the request for *Ahimsa* can lead to such heart-warming charity. Compassion and respect for life are considered not only as the most important prerequisites in any personal search for peace, harmony and honesty, but also form the basis for each human symbiosis with animals and nature. There is not the tiniest bit of ambiguity in the tenets expressed by Jain sages: Strictly forbidden are violation, abuse, suppression, enslavement, torture or the killing of fellow-creatures.

It might be for those reasons that not many Jain families keep a dog or cat as pet; in their opinion animals should not be locked up. Even sweets and chocolates in animal-forms are not eaten.

The demand for non-violence plays a main role also in the sector of nutrition. Killing, either as "sport" like hunting or as means of providing food, is inconceivable. Meat, fish and eggs are not allowed!

In order to enable the quest for non-violence to reach its widest scope, only certain kinds of fruits and vegetables are permitted. But even then some nuances have yet to be considered in that fruit from trees should be harvested preferably in a mature condition, if possible when it has fallen on the ground already. In this context the banana may be eaten, but the banana tree must stay intact and not be damaged by the harvesting process. Plants growing under the surface, like for example potatoes and carrots, are to be avoided because during their harvest not only animals might be injured but also the complete plant would be destroyed at the same time.

The required life of moderation and restraint demands that one refrains from cooking or eating after sunset, if at all possible. Regular periods of fasting are also to be observed. No gift of nature is to be used beyond the most urgent requirement; wastefulness is considered as abuse, if not even as theft. Furthermore excessive consumption leads to environmental pollution, which quite clearly is judged as a despicable act of aggression.

Ancient Wisdom Shows the Way

"Truth and Non-Violence are as old as Hills"

Mahatma Gandhi

The age-old demands for non-violence appear also in many Buddhist and Hindu scripts. This idea can certainly be regarded as a common spiritual heritage of mankind and shapes many philosophies - but it is nevertheless so very difficult to put into practice. The Jains show us a shining example for implementation by choosing an all encompassing respect for life as basis for their own well-being. So they manage in an impressive way to translate their convictions into everyday life actions - as a blessing for all.

The fact that such a philosophy of non-violence can melt away even seemingly insurmountable obstacles has been proven to the world by Mahatma Gandhi who described *Ahimsa* as the core of his personal outlook on life. In this connection it is worth mentioning that this Hindu, whose pacific actions changed the face of the world, had in fact been educated by a Jain monk.......

Distribution of the Jains Population in India (1971)

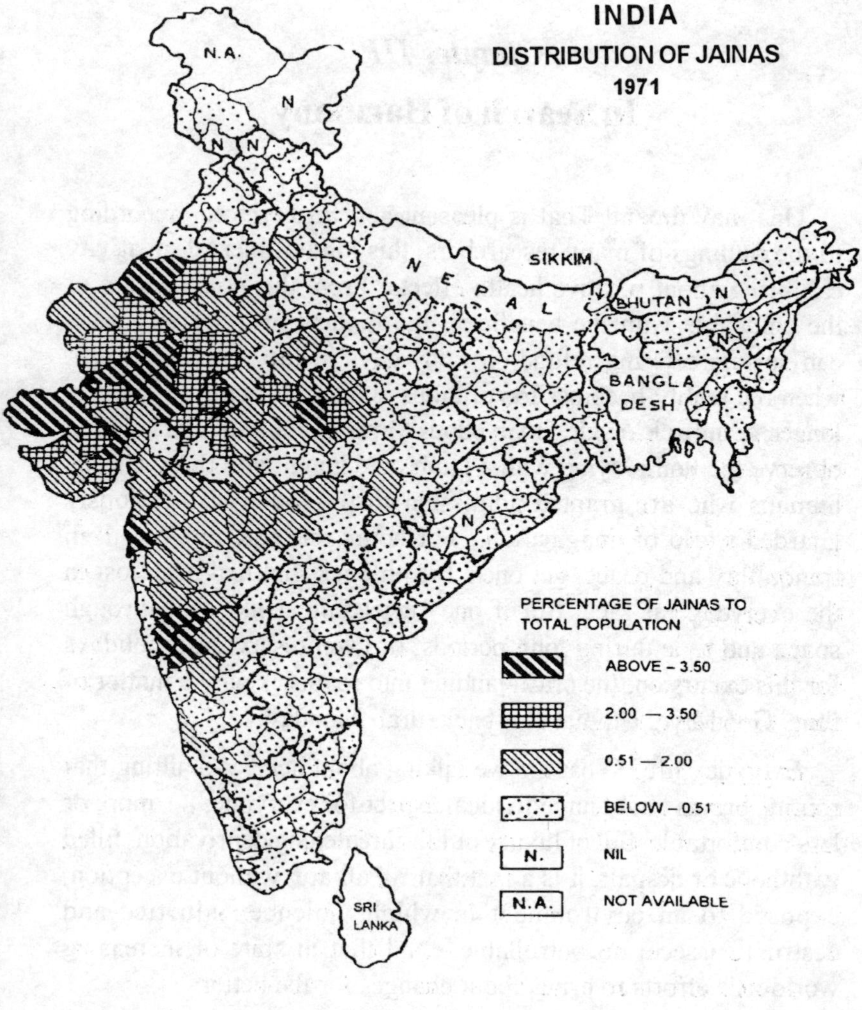

Chapter III

In Search of Harmony

One may dream! That is pleasant and furthermore, according to the findings of many researchers, this kind of mental creativity can bring about positive health effects. From this combination of the enjoyable with the beneficial, the fantasy of a secret garden can spring, offering refuge on rainy days in life. There one can, when the reality becomes too arduous and too difficult to face any longer, admire clear skies, marvellous forms and spectacular colours, observe the lion playing with a lamb, and laugh with those chosen humans who are granted admission to this otherwise jealously guarded world of imagination. For hours one can amble and, in tranquillity and peace, get one's breath back that had been lost in the everyday rat race. But if one keeps sailing like that through space and time during long periods, or even reserves all holidays for this excursion, the crash landing into reality is only a matter of time. Good-bye, Utopia! I'm back, drab Monday!

Everyday life? What are we talking about here? Admitting that routine brings about an individual aspect for everyone, i.e. more or less comfortable, full of luxury or life-threatening deprivation, filled with hope or despair, it is a fact that we all are, without exception, exposed to an environment in which violence, injustice and destruction seem uncontrollable - and that in spite of increasing worldwide efforts to bring about changes for the better.

There is no doubt that the initiatives everywhere in the interest of peace, human rights and justice are intensifying in momentum and urgency. We are all yearning for a new world with less suffering and misery but, nevertheless, a real break-through is not in view anywhere. A halfway pacified crisis in one part of the world is going to be followed by yet another conflict elsewhere that will break open with bloody force. All the efforts of researchers, scientists, military, institutes, organizations, diplomats and governments fail to bring more change than the remark of the frightened man, who, when watching the TV-news in the company of his wife, asks her a question that neither she nor anyone else knows the answer to: "Why do people do that?" Yes, indeed! Why?

What about the theory that with each bad deed the whole becomes a bit worse? And the contrary: that no good act is ever wasted? But those are theoretical considerations that one may accept or not and about which everyone will have his own opinion, just as everyone has chosen his own spiritual home.

But there are also practical considerations in this context because, after all, the Bishnois are the living proof that a loving and caring base of thought can bring about strong and positive consequences which can even turn out to be life-savers in critical situations.

Everyone knows that a desert has nothing in common with the Garden of Eden. And it is clear without detailed description how critical survival in such harsh areas can be in times of climatic disasters, above all drought. But these special desert people have accepted their environment, gave it all their attention, made peace with it and all the living beings in it. They created a harmony that allows them to carry on, whatever the circumstances.

Even if such a laborious everyday life does not appeal to us and seems not at all desirable, one must, however, not forget that the Bishnois have been able to develop a special kind of contact with nature and all its pulsations that we cannot sense any more. Never will we be allowed to experience the feeling of unity that a "wild" animal brings along when it approaches us voluntarily and trustingly.

The gentleness with which the Bishnois not only treat animals but also trees could help us also in preserving our forests, which become more vulnerable every year. According to official sources, the clearing of Brazilian tropical rain forests increased sharply in the year 2000. An area of record size was wiped clean of trees. By satellite pictures it can be demonstrated that in the year 2000 more than a half per cent (20,000 square kilometres) of the entire rain forest, the major part of which is situated in Brazil but also in the neighbouring states Venezuela and Colombia, was destroyed.

We ought not to saw off the branch on which, after all, we are all sitting. The destruction of the green lungs of Earth must stop if we do not want to pay a dangerously high price for our carelessness: an increasingly life-hostile climate.

However: the danger is quite well known! Numerous warnings have already been ignored! The felling goes on nevertheless without the slightest bit of restraint. Thus roaring chain saws everywhere continue, on a global scale, to destroy, within a few minutes, beautiful living beings which needed years (if not centuries!) to reach their current size and strength. Maybe one had better follow the advice of the tree squatter Julia Butterfly who said that each tree-cutter ought to live some years in a treetop before being allowed to destroy it. Or one takes the Bishnois as an example whose gratitude for trees and their blessings developed into a respect that does not allow destruction anymore.

Also the consideration of the Jains towards our non-human brothers is exemplary; especially since the ecological damages of an exploding cattle industry become more obvious everywhere and in most dramatic ways. In this context it seems interesting that in Switzerland more meat than bread is consumed today. To satisfy appetites like that ever more animals have to be raised - "from conception to the abattoir on a conveyer-belt"

But nature is at long last demonstrating the truly dramatic consequences of these "production processes": by flaming pyres of the corpses of millions of animals who have been culled in connection with BSE and other epidemics. Now even the most thick-skinned and greedy people are being made aware of the fact that changes must be made with the utmost urgency. After all, the animals belonging to what we call "life stock" have a right to care and dignity which we should better respect - and that not only in the interest of the animals! We have been made aware now that nature is infinitely patient but will not be manipulated eternally!

Is it really necessary in a country such as Belgium, with only 10 million inhabitants, that in just one single year the unbelievable number of 11 million pigs and additionally one million cattle and calves are slaughtered? If one adds other animals, such as poultry, the almost astronomical result of 225 millions dead animals was reached in the year 1998. And this concerns just one single country!

A forecast on world level shows the real extent of the blood bath that we create year in, year out - and that seems to be the most natural thing in the world, demanding not the slightest thought or feeling of guilt or sentiment of pity.

But it really does not need to be like this! The Jains have been living, so it is said in scriptures, already for thousands of years without meat. And they present themselves to the world as a solid, flourishing and wealthy community that has much to give and gives much. Their gentleness towards nature has brought about an impressive social result and shows at the same time that restraint does not necessarily mean grey asceticism and grim escapism. A good and successful life and active compassion with all living beings do go together extremely well - and for their most impressive living proof of this statement we owe gratitude to the Jains.

And in this perspective it shows that a long lasting and intensive respect for animals brings about at the same time a larger indulgence towards humans, as well as an overall noticeable reduction of aggressiveness and violence. If a community can be influenced by brutality and uncontrolled quest for power, so exactly the same holds true for the reverse: Pacific tendencies can still be reinforced by more peace. All it takes is to start and have the courage for the brave step. After all: there is always a first time for which it is never too late.

When we had the idea to write a book about vegetarian philosophies we did not know that we would find these mainly in India. It had not been our intention to concentrate on that nation in particular but our research led us rather quickly to that part of the world.

Certainly, there are other communities who live traditionally without meat but those in India are the oldest and largest. Maybe in a follow-on book project we could deal with another collection of vegetarian ways-of-life in other regions. We would be grateful for hints where these are to be found because, after all, we are convinced that Leonardo da Vinci was right in saying that the day will come when the killing of an animal will be seen as a big a crime as killing a human being. We want to look forward to this happy moment, even if today it has become a "reality" in our fantasies only.

CONTACTS

Jaina

Federation of Jains Associations in North America

www.jaina.org

JAINA Headquarters

P.O. Box 700

Getzville, NY 14068

E-mail: *jainahq@jaina.org*

Jain Association International (Germany) e. V.

24558 Henstedt-Ulzburg

Schweriner Str. 5

Germany

Website: *www.jain-germany.de*

E-Mail: *jain-germany@onlinehome.de*

Further Links

http://www.jainteerth.com/jainteerth/

http://www.jainsamaj.org/

Vegetarianism

Asian Vegetarian Union

114-A, Mittal Court

Nariman Point

Mumbai 400 021

India

Website: *www.ivu.org/avu/*

E-mail: *asia@ivu.org*

European Vegetarian Union (EVU)
Secretariat
26, Rue Moncoureur
B 7011 Ghlin
Belgium
Website: *www.european-vegetarian.org*
E-Mail: *evu@ivu.org*

International Vegetarian Union (IVU)
Parkdale
Dunham Road
Cheshire, WA14 4QG
UK
Website: *http://www.ivu.org /*
E-Mail: *chair@ivu.org*

Swiss Union for Vegetarianism
(Schweizerische Vereinigung fuer Vegetarismus)
Bahnhofstr. 52
CH 9315 Neukirch-Egnach
Switzerland
Website: *www.vegetarismus.ch*
E-mail: *svv@vegetarismus.ch*